Designing Exhibitions

Giles Velarde

WHITNEY LIBRARY OF DESIGN

an imprint of Watson-Guptill Publications/New York

First U.S. publication in 1989 in New York by
Whitney Library of Design
an imprint of Watson-Guptill Publications
a division of Billboard Publications, Inc.
1515 Broadway, New York, NY 10036

First published in Great Britain, 1988, by the Design Council

Designed by Ruth Prentice, assisted by Nicole Griffin

Library of Congress Cataloging-in-Publication Data

Velarde, Giles.
   Designing exhibitions.

   Bibliography: p.
   Includes index.
   1. Exhibitions. I. Title.
T396.5.V45   1989   659.1'52   88-20694

ISBN 0-8230-1326-X

Manufactured in Hong Kong

1 2 3 4 5 6 7 8 9 / 93 92 91 90 89 88

For Celia

CONTENTS

ACKNOWLEDGEMENTS

I am immensely grateful for the assistance of David Varley ARCA with the chapter 'The Words' and to Dennis Dyer with the chapter 'The Management'. Both of them are the best in their respective fields. I am also grateful for the chapter 'The Results' by Mick Alt. He was one of the first people to work in the field of evaluation in the UK and, while I respect the need for assessment of the type he writes about in his chapter, I could not possibly express it as well as he does. I am also grateful to John Furneaux and Laurie Stewart who opened their picture library to us: it has been an invaluable resource.

In 1980 I wrote a letter to James Woudhuysen, then Editor of *Design Magazine*, criticising the ignorance displayed in the writing of a recent article about exhibition design. A few weeks later I was invited to *Design* to discuss the possibility of more informed articles on the subject and to my surprise it was suggested that I should write a series of critical pieces about museum exhibitions up and down the country. James Woudhuysen's faith in my ability to do this was touching, and I embarked upon a secondary writing career with ever-increasing pleasure. I have managed to stay in print more or less continuously since that time, and I will always be grateful to him for that start.

In September 1985 I spent a happy few hours showing two Frenchmen around a new exhibition at the Geological Museum in London, explaining some of the complex techniques that had been used to communicate the detailed information. At the end of our time together they pressed me to write a book about exhibitions. I took this as a compliment, but it set me thinking. Completely separately, a month later the Design Council approached me with the suggestion that I submit a proposal for a book, which I did. In the spring of 1986 I went to the Réserve Géologique in Digne, Haute Provence — from where my two visitors had come — and gave a series of lectures. It was these lectures which gave me the basis upon which to build the book. I am therefore most grateful to Guy Martini and Alexandre Maucoronel, the Director and Chief Technician of the Réserve Géologique in Digne, for giving me the confidence and opportunity to gather my thoughts before writing.

Finally, nothing would be possible without the constant support of my wife, Celia, to whom this book is firmly dedicated. It is she who takes the spare 'l' out of my familly, puts the 'm' in my accomodation, and the commas and verbs in my rambling sentences. Without her, this book would not exist.

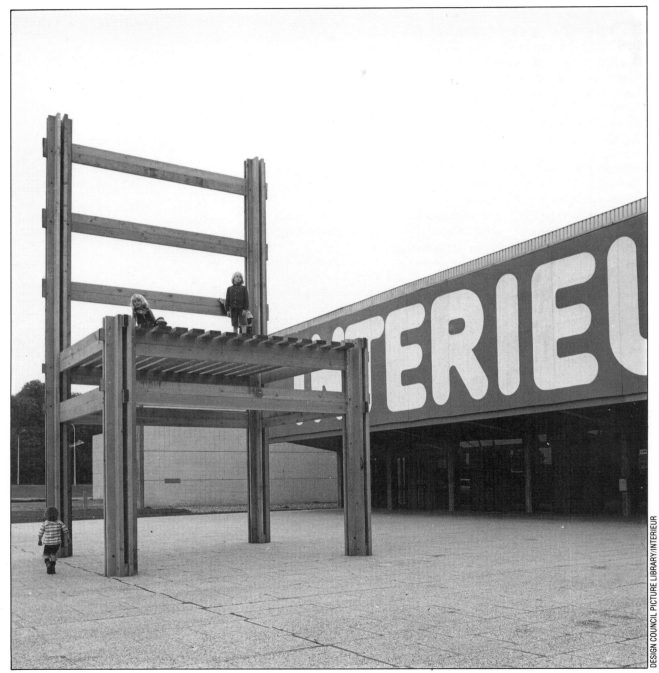

FOREWORD

Exhibitions are at best magic, and at worst dreary trudges around gloomy trade shows or museums. The purveyance of magic is, of course, a serious business. Despite this, most people go to exhibitions in the expectation of having a good time — there is no reason why they should not — but it is easy to design or formalise the pleasure out of an exhibition and end up with something which, while fulfilling the basic requirements, remains a sterile and unprepossessing display. The magic element therefore, after people have been persuaded to go in the first place, is to enlighten and, hopefully, entertain them at the same time.

It is possible in the generally indoor world of exhibitions to erect wonderful structures with essential facts communicated through marvellous illusions, but these illusions should never dominate the information. The style should never overpower the message, nor the personality of the designer ride rough-shod over the exhibitor.

Exhibiting things is an ancient profession. There is very little difference between the money-lenders Jesus Christ found in the temple two thousand years ago, and the Business Efficiency Exhibition at Olympia. Moral values may have changed; the construction will certainly be different; but on both occasions the exhibition was there to persuade the public to buy the services on offer. In fact, the basic considerations were identical. The physical constraints were dictated by the place and the characteristics of the people involved, and people were 'selling' to people.

Selling is often seen to be an ugly word, but it is what an exhibition is for. In simple terms, the commercial exhibition stand is designed to sell a product and the museum exhibition is to sell ideas. Both activities make certain basic demands: they must attract visitors, they must hold the visitor's attention and they must inform the visitor. In the first example they must persuade the visitor to buy, and in the second to want to know more.

While dividing exhibition production into a number of obvious categories which form the chapter headings of this book, it would also be possible to divide the process laterally under the basic demands mentioned above (to attract, to hold, to inform, to persuade), but this would lead to a complex format and impossibly complicated chapters. It is nevertheless important to remember that the first nail and the last word are all part of the communication process generally described as exhibition design.

No attempt has been made to differentiate between commercial and non-commercial exhibitions, for the author can see no fundamental difference. While many museum exhibitions are permanent, as many are temporary. Though most museum exhibitions are simply informative, they would be useless if no one visited them, stayed for a while, learned something and went away enlightened. They must sell themselves. While many commercial exhibitions are simply for indirect selling, the same criteria apply and a huge number of informative and prestige exhibitions are simply for enlightenment or information. Whether the materials in one exhibition might have to last twenty years and in another twenty days, they are dealing with the same commodities: information, people and space. The commerical and museum fields, therefore, are hopelessly intertwined and, although the museologist might dismiss the Motor Show as trade and the car salesman might regard the museum as fuddy-duddy, they are both actually doing the same thing.

Materials and fittings are an area of danger in a book of this kind: it would date very rapidly if exact types of material or fixings were to be quoted constantly. These materials vary and evolve continuously. The norms of twenty years ago and today are completely different, as indeed they will be in twenty years' time. This book, therefore, ignores specific materials as much as possible and attempts to aim at broad principles, descriptions and methods. It is hoped that this book will help the reader in the process of exhibition production, but whereas the first nail has been mentioned as a starting point, there is no attempt to specify the type of nail or where it should be put.

The little sister of exhibition design is display design, often called p.o.s. or point of sale design. In order to clarify the terminology, the word 'display' will be used a great deal. Display is what takes place in an exhibition. There will be many displays in an exhibition and the process of mounting an exhibition is often referred to as 'putting on a display'. But this book does not deal with p.o.s. design in any way, for that is a field exclusive to shops or points of direct sale. You can rarely walk away from a commercial exhibition with an object — only the desire or intent to buy one. There are probably books about p.o.s. design, and there are certainly many courses in colleges and polytechnics. Not so with exhibitions. There are very few books, and only one known full-time course on the subject at the time of writing. The problem is that such a wide area of design knowledge is required to design an exhibition successfully that the ideal training is certainly degree level and most probably post-graduate level. For some reason this is not yet on offer in the colleges of the United Kingdom.

All design should be a thoughtful process; to be a good designer is to be an acute observer and understander of people, who can use this observation and understanding to serve certain ends. Design is also the manipulation of style, taste, colour, tone, shape, form and decoration to make something that will perform a function. Many people believe that if an object performs its function well, it will have an intrinsic beauty. 'Form follows function' is the phrase emanating from Bauhaus days which sums this up, and it is hard to look at a satisfactory hand tool, sailing boat or vehicle without seeing the sense in it.

But the function can only be properly fulfilled if the designer has thought about the solution to the problem. If he becomes obsessed with expressions of his own taste and style, and injections of his own personality, the design will fail.* It may receive transient acclaim, but it will play no part in the advancement of knowledge and the improvement of life. Exhibitions, no matter how temporary, can be part of that essential progress. If their function is to sell something, then there is nothing wrong with that — unless they fail.

In the process of designing, interaction between the designer and contractors, carpenters, technicians, sales and business people, managers, painters, electricians, bureaucrats and scientists is essential. These interactions are enhanced if the designer keeps a cool head and remembers that all of them are people with problems, pressures, aspirations and dreams, just like him-or herself. It costs nothing to be polite and thoughtful. It will massively benefit the whole process, and therefore, inevitably, the end result.

This book is based on the wide experience of one person, fed by the knowledge and experience of others all along the line; particularly by seven years spent with the exhibition designer and architect, Arthur Braven. To those early days, trotting in and out of contractors' workshops and meeting specialist craftspeople with whom the author has worked very happily over many years, a great deal is owed, and their names now fill a large address book.

The address book of any exhibition designer is his or her most valuable possession, so it is humbly hoped that this book might find a place somewhere near it.

*Wherever possible, sole use of the masculine pronoun has been avoided, except where its avoidance would make a clumsy construction.

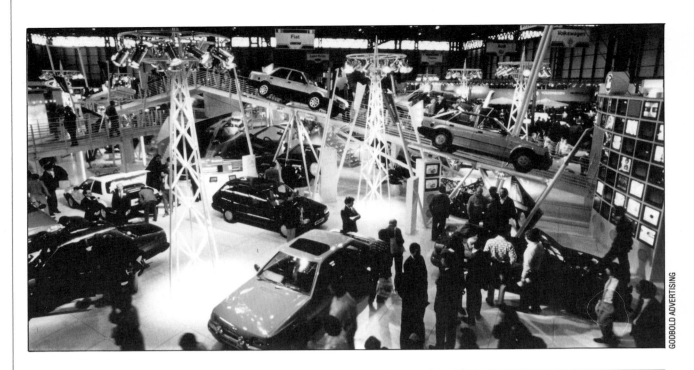

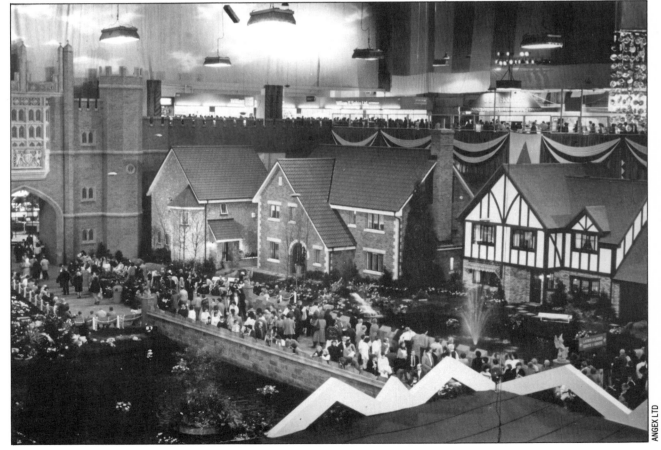

1

THE EXHIBITION

Exhibitions come in all shapes and sizes. Resultantly, they mean many different things to different people. It is not even possible to be too specific about what the word 'exhibition' means, as it is one of those words which have several public meanings and even more 'professional' ones. It is a semantic jungle into which we must advance rapidly, or this book will never get started.

To deal with the public meaning first: it is generally used for exhibitions of paintings or shows, such as the Motor Show or the Ideal Home Exhibition. Nevertheless, it is so much associated in the public mind with paintings that many an exhibition designer has been asked over the gin and tonic if he or she arranges the paintings and the lighting. Surprisingly enough, at the time of writing, this is the one area of exhibition design still dominated by amateurs.

Exhibitions, shows, displays, fairs are all words used to mean the same sort of thing when exhibition professionals communicate with each other. The first exhibitions were probably displays of goods for sale on market stalls. Even in those simple circumstances, efforts were and still are made to display things in such a way that people are encouraged to move close and admire them. But what are they admiring? The beautifully stacked apples or pears, or the beautiful stacking in a neat, orderly arrangement? Is the stall holder doing it to please himself (or hide the back of the fruit which is rotten) or to attract the buyer? In that peculiar seller/buyer relationship, it is undoubtedly done to sell more, and the stall holder knows it. So the ancient and effective market stall, now thousands of years old and still going, has evolved to the technically sophisticated razzamatazz of the Motor Show and, in the meantime, has spawned trade fairs, world fairs, eco-centres, heritage centres, contemporary museum galleries and exhibitions, science centres and travelling exhibitions of one sort or another.

The exquisite market stall remains commonplace throughout the world, and indeed that type of display can still be found in the marble halls of Harrods in London. Chinese pavilions at world and trade fairs specialise in arrangements where quantity, and therefore presumed quality, are the only message. But exhibitions have to be separated out from stalls and shops as the former are very rarely associated with direct sales. The whole purpose of an exhibition is to persuade people of the good quality of a product; to make them consider purchasing, rather than actually purchase.

◄ **General view of the Motor Show, National Exhibition Centre, Birmingham, 1987.**

◄ **Central feature of the Ideal Home Exhibition, 1987.**

For this reason, commercial exhibitions have evolved into high pressure events where most of the selling is done by salespeople to salespeople. Wholesalers therefore persuade retailers to buy and sell on, in possibly another form, to a customer sometimes way down at the end of the line. These exhibitions therefore are often completely removed from an end product. Plastics, for instance, in their crudest form, along with detailed specifications of their properties, could be sold to a manufacturer who might only make part of a product which is passed on to another assembler, who might make the final product to sell to you or me.

Of course, as soon as information is brought in beside the product, things start to get complicated. Words take up space; people reading them take up even more space. Pictures and diagrams are needed as part of the explanation. Pictures need space and if many pictures are required, where will the space come from? Slide shows emerge, so why not have a spoken commentary? So the contemporary exhibition begins to emerge, more and more remote from the eventual customer — except of course in museums or heritage centres. Here the line of communication is direct. In any such display the 'curator' should be trying to communicate directly with the actual user. There is no intermediary here; the basic circumstances are as primitive as the market stall. While museums might fulfil similar purposes, they have to employ much more subtle means to reach so many different types of visitor.

Displaying to sell; displaying to delight; displaying to persuade — all perhaps achieving enlightenment, too — deal with the same basic commodity: three-dimensional, informative space.

TRADE FAIRS

These demonstrate exhibitions in the widest possible variety, from the simple stall to the multi-decked, island site, exhibition stand. Some background information is therefore required. Trade fairs take place all over the world, all the time. At any given moment, there will be at least one trade fair going on somewhere. These are exhibitions established for manufacturers and are frequently categorised. Book fairs, food fairs, motor spares fairs, cycle shows, computer shows, business efficiency exhibitions — practically everything has its own trade fair. They are the exhibitions at which the various trades meet to sell components to each other, to catch up with the competition, to buy components and, as often as not, to have a good night out with the boys or girls. The public is rarely invited, and barely knows they are going on. Huge halls exist in major and minor cities of the world. In London we have Olympia and Earls Court. The National Exhibition Centre is near Birmingham. Most of the halls are purpose built; some are adapted from their original purpose (the Business Design Centre in Islington was formerly an agricultural exhibition hall). Usually the buildings are owned by a local council or a limited company, and space inside is let to

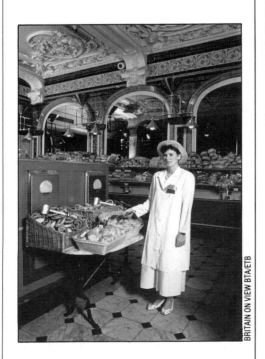

▲ **Harrods Food Hall.**

BRITAIN ON VIEW BTA/ETB

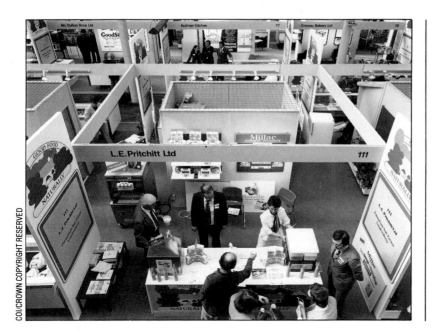

◀ A typical trade fair.

▼ National Exhibition Centre, Birmingham.

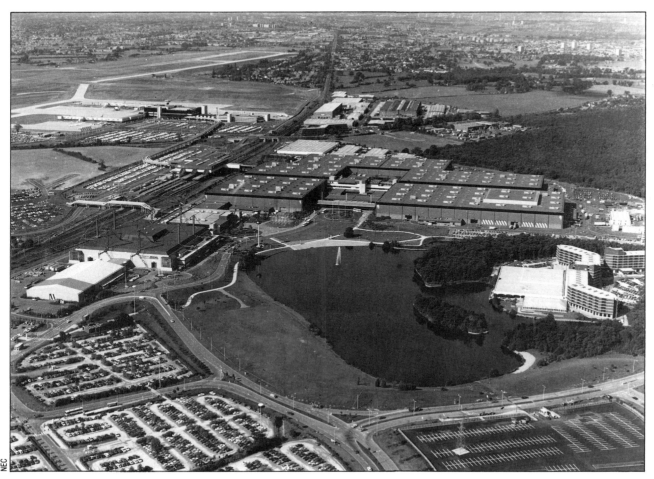

15

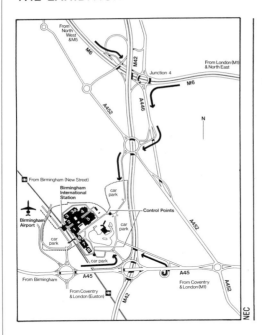

exhibitors in packages of square feet or metres. These are allocated along predetermined aisles.

The usual procedure is for a scheme of booths, stalls or stands to be let out on a first come, first served basis. The plan is normally arranged to accommodate a simple structure called a 'shell scheme'. This is an empty stall of a consistent size, possibly four metres deep by four wide, with thin board walls papered and painted white, an adequate floor covering, sometimes an 80–100 mm platform. A board perhaps 400 or 500 mm deep is put across the front of the stall to carry a name, and behind it will be simple, adequate lighting. The walls are suitable for supporting panels or lightweight objects. This very simple box can be hired for the duration of the show, and it is quite possible with careful

◀ **National Exhibition Centre, Birmingham. Superb communications but Olympia and Earls Court in London still have a powerful appeal.**

▼ **Government information stand, National Exhibition Centre, Birmingham.**

Notice that the people on both these exhibitions stands are as important as the displays.

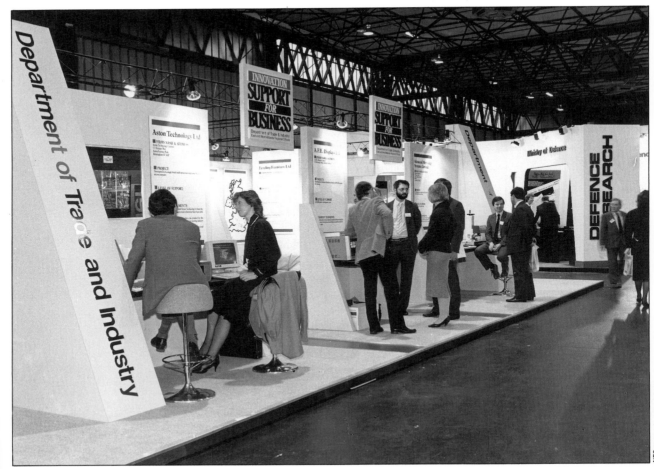

design to turn it into something very attractive. It is also often possible to request the organisers for the space only and design an exhibition stand oneself. The advantage is that, of course, there is a great deal more control and, provided the organisers' regulations and the neighbours are respected, a much more dynamic presentation can be attempted. The aim of the latter enterprise is to separate distinctly the company or organisation from its neighbours, to accommodate special exhibits or displays, and generally have greater control over the expensive piece of territory which has been rented.

With a greater outlay of money it is generally possible to buy an island site and build an exhibition stand. Again, the rules of the organisers must be accepted, but frequently they allow for the construction of quite exotic structures. Double deckers have an extra floor which doubles the exhibition space. In this kind of enterprise, it is not only the rules of the organisers that must be considered, but also local or national government regulations concerning safety. Structures which support people over the heads of others must of course be soundly built, fire-resistant and offer clear means of escape; but it is still possible under those

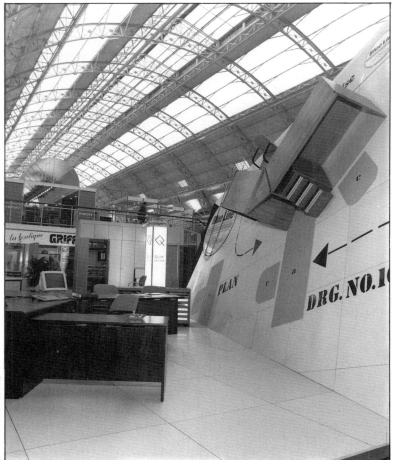

BUSINESS DESIGN CENTRE

◄ **London's most recent conversion for trade fairs and the like – the Business Design Centre in Islington. The recent reopening of this nineteenth-century agricultural show hall has had a marvellous effect on the whole neighbourhood.**

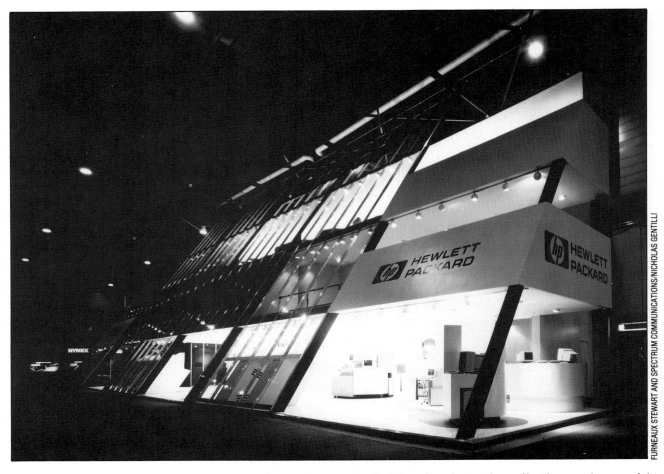

FURNEAUX STEWART AND SPECTRUM COMMUNICATIONS/NICHOLAS GENTILLI

▲ **A double decker by Furneaux Stewart for Hewlett Packard. By going on to two floors the designers have increased the available floor space from 350 to 854 square metres.**

circumstances to build quite fantastic, effective and graceful structures which will enormously enhance a product and provide a superb showcase for new products or special developments.

It is most important when considering exhibiting within a shell scheme-based trade fair to try and pick a site at the earliest possible moment. There are many factors affecting the selection. A site looking down an aisle is clearly going to be noticed by many more people than a site lost halfway down a raggle-taggle of identical booths. Corner sites and sites facing the entrance to a trade fair are obviously in prime positions, as are island sites. An outside corner site naturally has less walls for display, but it commands more aisle. A site below windows on the outer wall of a hall can be poorly positioned, as it is hard to compete with daylight, particularly when the sun is low. The one thing over which there is no control is choice of neighbour; but as soon as this is known it is as well to get in touch and come to terms over conflicting displays (which are only two inches apart at the edge of the stand area). Another important factor affecting site selection is the presence of heavy or bulky exhibits; if these are involved it is vital not only to have a site which can accommodate

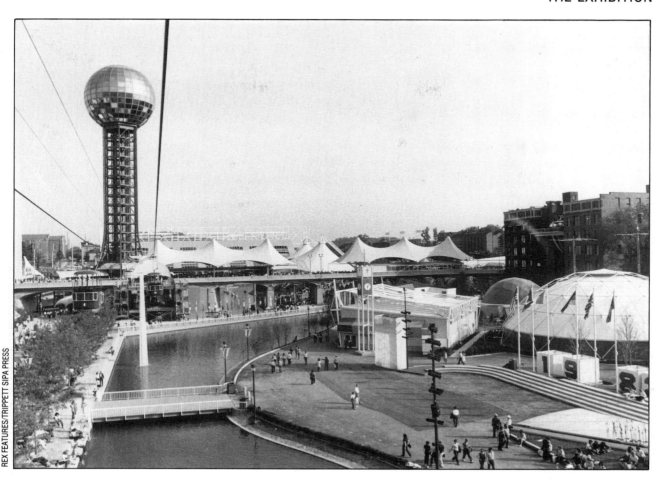

them but also adequate aisles and headroom to facilitate lifting machinery.

Frequently, exhibitors choose their own sites without reference to designers. Of course some exhibitors are experienced pickers, but some are not, and it is as well to involve the designer from the outset to ensure that a thoroughly useable site within the allocated budget is chosen.

▲ **The Sunsphere, Knoxville World Fair, 1982. All world fairs seem to be dominated by massive vertical features.**

WORLD FAIRS

Many a city with a dynamic Mayor and a go-ahead Chamber of Commerce has considered the possibility of having a world fair. There is in fact an international organisation in Paris[1] specifically set up to control the displacement of such fairs around the world, though in recent years they seem to have proliferated in North America and Japan. They come in 'classes' which denote size, regularity and characteristics. Those that remain in our memories are generally the Class 1: super-colossal fairs such as Montreal in 1967 or Osaka in 1970. The more common are smaller specialised fairs. Small is a relative term, however. The fair in Knoxville in 1982 set out to achieve perhaps half a million visitors a month, and actually achieved double that for its six-

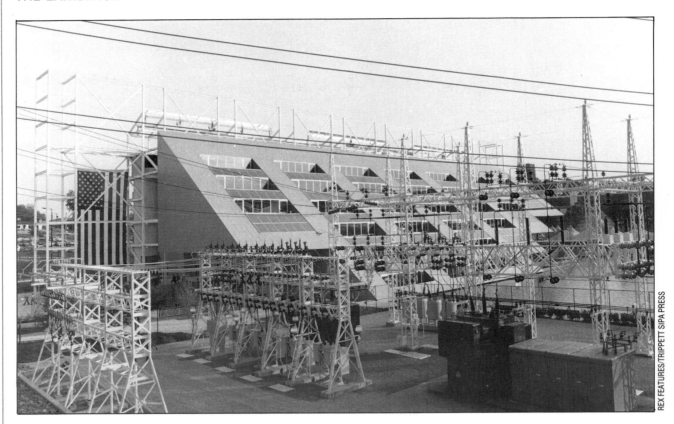

▲ **US Pavilion, Knoxville World Fair, 1982. This pavilion was retained as a research facility for Knoxville University. There are frequently long-term, local benefits to be gained from short-term fairs of this kind.**

▶ **Toshiba Pavilion, Expo '67, Montreal.**

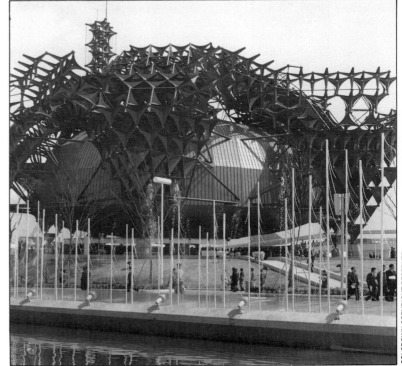

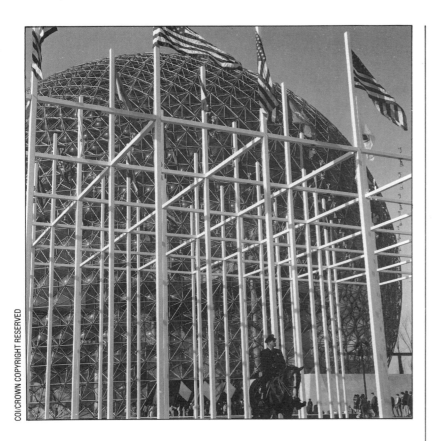

◄ US Pavilion, Expo '67, Montreal. Buckminster Fuller's startling contribution to 1960s architecture.

month summer stint. Knoxville was very successful, so it is perhaps a good example to describe.

In the late 1970s a dynamic local businessman and member of the Chamber of Commerce decided that the economy of that romantically named Tennessee town needed a lift. The City Council had, in the middle of the town, a derelict waste land with all its attendant problems. There was a disused mill and station, a swamp and rubbish tip, all crying out for redevelopment. What better than a world fair to focus attention on Knoxville's charms and facilities, as well as cleaning up the town? The comprehensive and well-drafted proposal for a world-class fair was presented to the World Fair Headquarters in Paris and eventually sanctioned. Invitations were sent out under the theme of 'World Energy Resources' (the Tennessee River Authority has its headquarters near Knoxville) and 21 major countries agreed to participate. The parent country, the USA, would gain national prestige by building a magnificent pavilion which would remain as a permanent research facility for the University of Knoxville. The EEC submitted a bid for a combined pavilion and they, like all the other major countries participating, were allocated space in specially constructed temporary industrial buildings. Australia, Canada, China, Hungary and South Korea were among the other participants. A committee was formed, architects appointed, volunteers co-opted and an administrative office

▶ **London's Chelsea Flower Show, 1982. Most people who visit this show are not really aware that they are at an exhibition.**

▶ **The Boat Show, Earls Court 1988. The massive and rarely used swimming pool comes into its own once a year.**

established. The derelict site was landscaped and rapidly transformed into a park. The swamp became a lake, the old mill and station were refurbished and added a touch of old-fashioned class to the site. One end of the park was transformed into a funfair with the biggest ferris wheel in the world. Concessions for restaurants, hamburger stalls, novelty shops and boutiques were granted. Eventually the foreign participants arrived, took over the empty sheds and transformed them into air-conditioned palaces of national prestige. Meanwhile a sunsphere, containing a revolving restaurant, was jacked a hundred feet up a trellis steel column to provide the obligatory landmark invented by Monsieur Eiffel a hundred years before. Audiovisual displays and electronic gadgetry abounded; an IMEX cinema was constructed to serve the American pavilion and various giant corporations built their own pavilions.

In April 1982 hundreds of pavilion managers, designers, shopkeepers, restaurant managers and fair organisers stood anxiously by their posts as the gates were opened. They need not have worried — the sums had been right. The first visitors swarmed into the pristine park and within a few hours the hosts to the huge crowd knew they had a success on their hands. The timing, the site, the theme, the weather — all were perfect. For Britain the Falklands factor was having its effect and large queues grew to visit the British section of the EEC pavilion, with the Germans the best of a dull bunch. The very longest queue, standing for three hours in tropical heat, was for the Chinese pavilion; but the Australian pavilion, which had nothing to recommend it but brilliant design, slowly built up enormous popularity. Their formula was exactly right: a simple story line, text at the right levels and easy movement inside the pavilion which had two entrances and exits. The whole thing was a triumph of experience applied to good design and management.

What did Knoxville get out of it? Six months of free-spending tourists (a million a month); the fine USA pavilion as a boost to the University; a park instead of a derelict site and a huge lift to the economy of the town and region. The commercial exhibitors, the national pavilions and the city benefited from the international publicity. Suffice it to say that Knoxville considered it well worth their while to embark on the project, and although the New Orleans World Fair two years later was not a commercial success, there seems to be a never-ending cycle of them.

PUBLIC TRADE SHOWS

These exhibitions, usually annual events with massive attendance figures, frequently start with a day or two devoted to the press and trade visitors only. After this, they throw their doors open to the paying public. Some, like the Boat Show in London's Earls Court at Christmas, are seasonal events without which the year would not seem quite complete. The Ideal Home Exhibition in the spring is another very popular exhibition, clogging up the streets of West London for a whole month. The Chelsea Flower

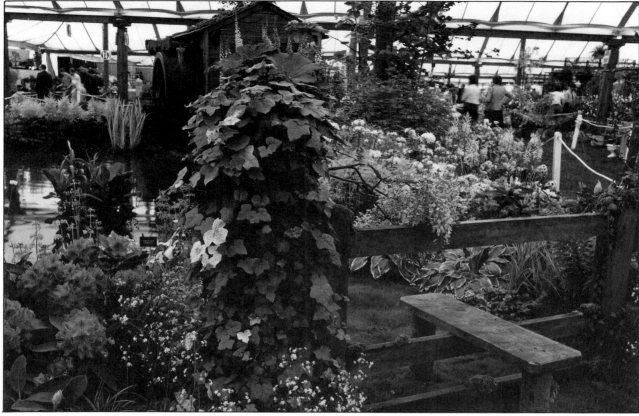

HARRY SMITH COLLECTION

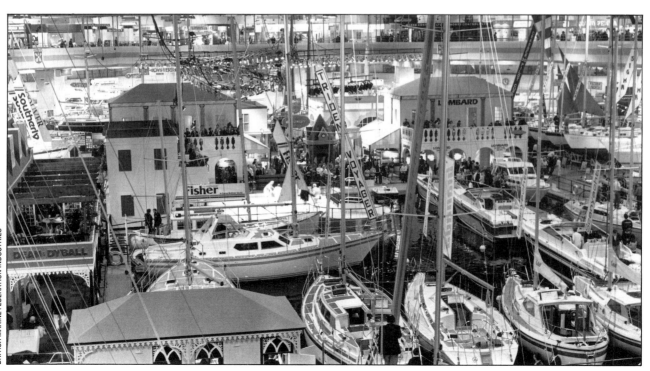

BRITISH MARINE FEDERATION INDUSTRIES

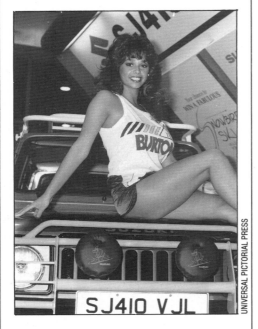

UNIVERSAL PICTORIAL PRESS

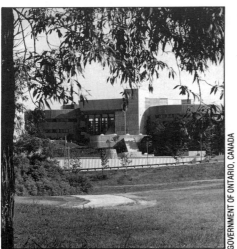

GOVERNMENT OF ONTARIO, CANADA

▲ ▲ **Who is selling what at this Motor Show?**

▲ **Ontario Science Centre, Toronto, now serves as a guide to state and national organisations embarking on ventures of this kind.**

Show, regularly attended by the Queen, has the same effect on that part of the city, but for a shorter time — cut flowers being what they are. The Royal Show, a great agricultural exhibition held in a specially designated and facilitated setting at Stoneleigh in Warwickshire, mixes exhibits with competitions, while in the autumn the Motor Show, either at Earls Court or the NEC near Birmingham, is another seasonal landmark. Because of the massive public presence at these shows, the by-laws governing stand construction and fireproofing are very strict. This does not hinder the creation of some very exotic structures. At the Boat Show, the normally hidden swimming pool is uncovered and filled with water to provide a suitably aquatic stage in which to float the most eye-catching boats and around which to build an exotic setting, reproducing some far-off resort and harbour. Fashion parades are held on this central feature, while beyond are thousands of square metres of more conventional display space, often sporting yachts and power boats too big to be floated in the pool. Some of the boats shown here are among the biggest exhibits ever seen on dry land. The exhibition is built around them after they have been manoeuvred into the near-empty hall. Apart from this, and its central feature, the Boat Show is fairly conventional. Boats are such compelling exhibits that very little is needed to emphasise their charms. Cars, however, which should come into that category, seem to bring out the greatest excesses in display — as they often do with their drivers — and while it is enormous fun for a male exhibition designer to see pretty, near-naked girls draped over highly polished coupés on press day, it is hard to see what they have to do with cars. (Nothing, though a great deal to do with selling.) This is of course what leads to the phenomenally costly methods of display used in these promotions; mirrored revolves and tilts, multiscreen audiovisual projections, specially made cutaways, animated models and so on. It is easy to deride these lavish expenditures, but out of them just occasionally comes a development of real value to exhibition designers in other areas of the profession.

— SCIENCE CENTRES, HERITAGE AND ECO-CENTRES —

In the early 1960s Philips Industries at Eindhoven decided to celebrate their then prime position in lighting and communications electronics by building a permanent exhibition explaining the field of technology to the ordinary Dutchman in the street. They built, what was for the time, a fantastic mushroom of a building and employed the English designer, James Gardner, to design the exhibition itself. It is justly and internationally famous to this day. Ahead of its time, it became a model and guide for the building of such establishments as the Ontario Science Centre in Toronto and the Exploratorium in San Francisco. Meanwhile, throughout the western world the conservation lobby has made us more and more aware of the importance and value of our surroundings. Information centres with permanent or semi-permanent exhibitions are being built in or near areas of historical

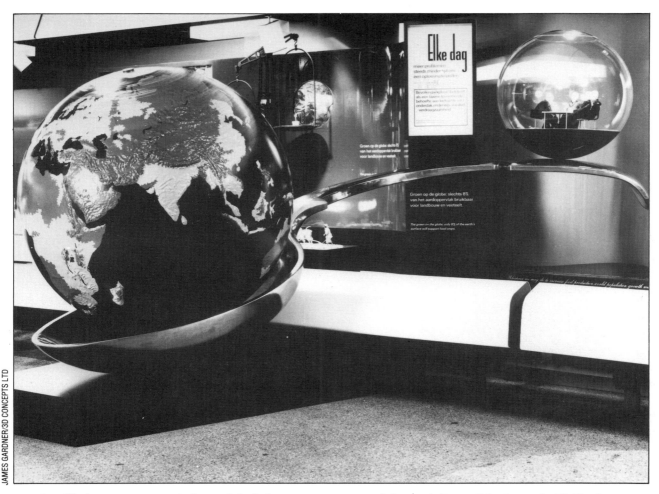

JAMES GARDNER/3D CONCEPTS LTD

▲ **Part of Evoluon, the Philips'
permanent exhibition at Eindhoven
in the Netherlands, designed by
James Gardner.**

or scientific interest to remind us of their importance, to explain their value and often to raise money to preserve them. Where these are built in a town or village they are generally called heritage centres, and in rural surroundings they are often called eco- or ecology centres.

Heritage centres usually consist of a building which is preserved in its own right with the exhibition built into it. Displays and tableaux of life in and around the village or town, artefacts, documents, old film and photographs are woven into displays, large and small. Obviously, the generally ancient buildings in which these displays are housed have to be respected; building an exhibition inside an exhibit is no mean task. Frequently the work is undertaken in conjunction with a specialist architect, and it is as well if the designer and the architect are brought together from the start, and not at the last moment, long after important decisions about lighting, power supply, ventilation and access should have been taken. Eco-centres specialise in presenting the countryside to the interested visitor. Near the Camargue in the South of France, for example, is the famous Musée Camarguais, the work of a team of designers led by Georges Henri de la

Rivière, essentially devoted to explaining man's involvement with the region. Deep in the heart of the Camargue itself is the Réserve Nationale du Camargue, devoted entirely to explaining the natural history and wildlife of the area. The public is given a varied presentation in a modern exhibition, the centrepiece of which is a television camera permanently monitoring the life of birds in a nest. There is a lecture theatre and facilities for school parties. A hundred miles away, up in the mountains of Haute Provence at Digne, there is a geological reserve where a fine exhibition explains the geology of the dramatic scenery and its effect upon the flora and fauna. The design, construction and

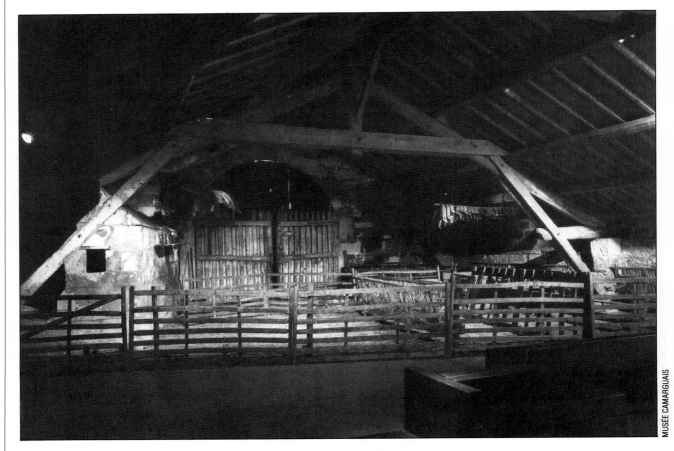

MUSÉE CAMARGUAIS

▲ **The Camargue Museum in the South of France. The old sheep fold is now a fine regional museum. This interior view shows the museum's original use.**

installation of these displays is all exhibition work, and can be a real challenge to the designer involved.

MUSEUMS

The line between contemporary science, as described in the last paragraph, and historical information, is so thin in some museums as to be invisible. Museums in the public mind, however, are generally associated with the past. Since the late 1960s the word 'museum' has lost its old-fashioned connotation. 'Museum piece' is no longer the derogatory term it used to be. One of the first

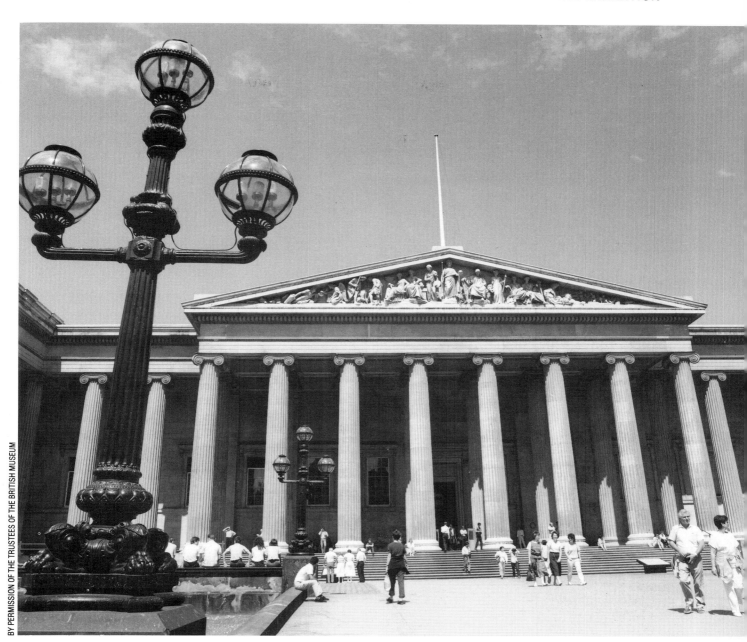

▲ The British Museum. Along with its massive permanent collections, its own design team has produced an enthralling sequence of temporary exhibitions, starting with the Tutankhamun Exhibition in 1972.

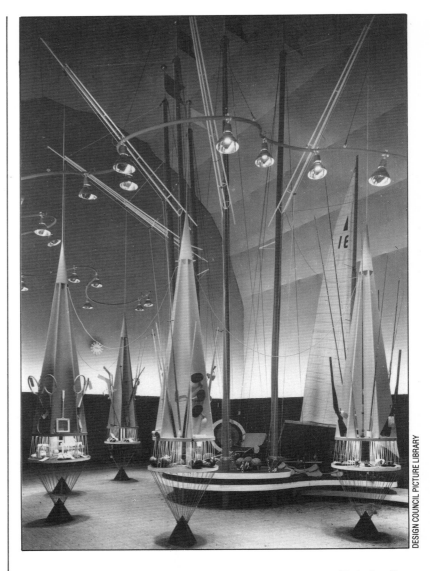

DESIGN COUNCIL PICTURE LIBRARY

► **The sport and leisure section of the 'Britain Can Make It' exhibition of 1946. Designed by James Gardner and Basil Spence. Displays by Robert Gordon.**

major exhibitions to take place in a museum was 'Britain Can Make It' in the Victoria & Albert (which itself grew out of the Great Exhibition of 1851), designed by James Gardner in 1946. This was a milestone in exhibition design and helped to put the profession on the map. While a few distinguished exhibitions took place in museums in the UK after that, it was not until the Tutankhamun Exhibition, designed by Margaret Hall, opened in the British Museum in 1972 that the British public really caught hold of the idea that museums could be places of fun.

Shortly after that, in the same year, 'The Story of the Earth', which was a permanent exhibition in the Geological Museum — again designed by James Gardner — opened and the public realised that even exhibitions of natural science could be exciting and interesting. It was always taken for granted that the Science Museum would be fun, since there were so many interactive

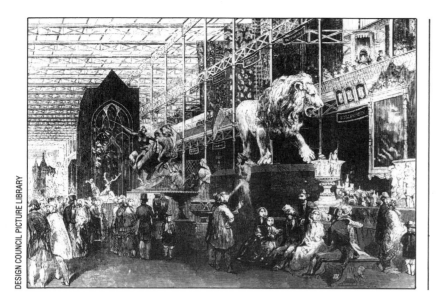

◀ The Great Exhibition of 1851, certainly not the first exhibition in the world but very much the beginning of what might be described as the modern type of popular exhibition.

▼ James Gardner's 'Story of the Earth' exhibition at London's Geological Museum, 1972.

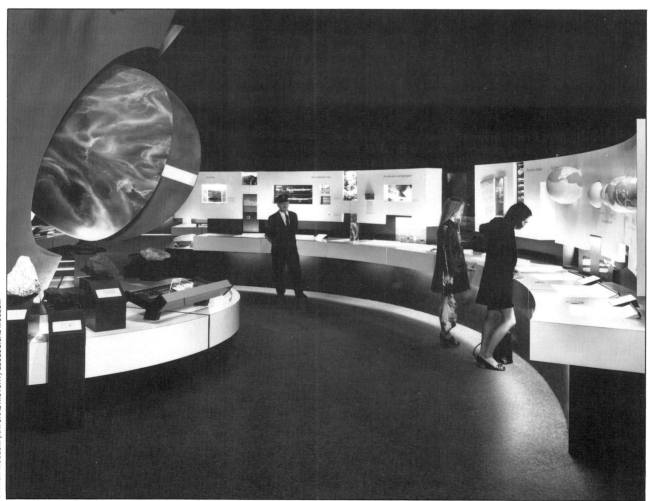

displays there; but until that time it had not been considered possible that the public could interact with an exhibition about geology. These major developments sparked off a rebirth of museum interest. Designers were called in, where previously curators and draughtsmen had cobbled together displays. In the Natural History Museum, for example, an entire department — the Department of Public Services — was set up to formulate a policy for interpreting natural sciences to the public. Designers and technicians began to be employed on a permanent basis in national and provincial museums. Across the Atlantic, in Canada and the USA, similar developments were taking place. Here an early emphasis was on exhibit evaluation. Commercial marketing and psychological experiments were done in an attempt to find out exactly how much people learned from exhibits. In the Milwaukee Museum, extensive research programmes were set up under Professor Chan Screven of the University Psychology Department, and several papers have emerged from that source on exhibit evaluation before production, during an exhibition, and after it is over.

So museums are now places for exhibitions: some permanent, often referred to as galleries; some temporary. Permanent constructions of course demand higher standards of both content and construction than temporary exhibitions, but both frequently deal with precious or irreplaceable objects so the difference need not be too great. Higher standards of content are necessary quite simply because it will receive far greater scrutiny than a temporary structure. An immortalised mistake can be pretty hard to live with. The reason for higher standards of construction is evident. Both sorts of museum exhibition, as indeed that in the following paragraph, may require security and conservation to be taken into account. There is a comprehensive work (*The Manual of Curatorship*, now in its second edition) and experts on both these subjects which the ignorant (and that includes the author) are advised to consult when the need arises (see Bibliography).

ART GALLERIES

As previously mentioned, this is the one group of exhibitions still dominated by the amateur. In national galleries, there is a body of curatorial expertise which still dictates the displacement of pictures in an exhibition. The word 'interpretation' is unfamiliar to them in the exhibition context, and the effective movement of people through space is not even a consideration. Clearly, if the exhibition of paintings is on a theme, this will emanate from the curator, but when considerations of planning, labelling, lighting and general display are dominated by non-designers it will be to the detriment of the exhibition. Sadly, this often goes unremarked by the press who visit the exhibition on preview day under exclusive and less crowded circumstances than the public, who have never been led to expect anything better. In fact, badly or non-designed exhibitions of paintings are commonplace. The public will put up with horrendous conditions: overcrowded gal-

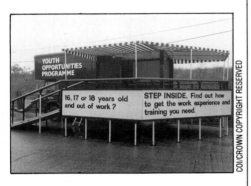

▲ A mobile exhibition. All the visible structure can be dismantled easily and placed inside the lorry for transit.

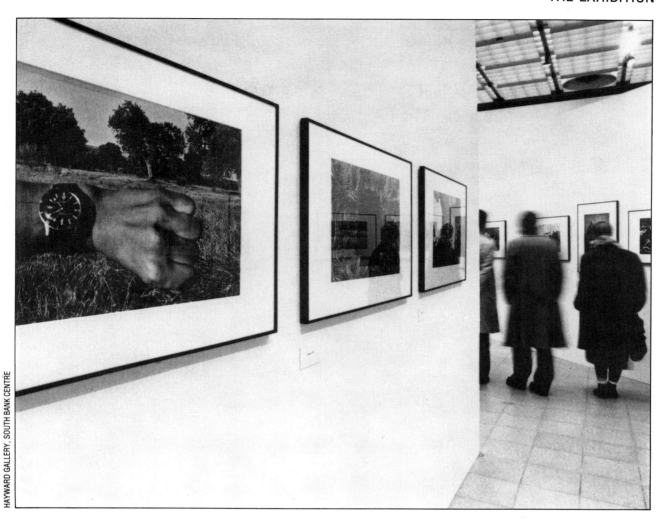

HAYWARD GALLERY, SOUTH BANK CENTRE

leries, bottlenecks and voids. These are generally accompanied by terse, badly positioned labels in too-small typefaces, demanding a to-and-fro movement between the pictures' viewing distance and the labels' reading distance, sometimes up to ten metres. At the time of writing, designers when used in art galleries seem to be employed simply to decorate. It is hoped that one day they will be allowed to design.

▲ **Josef Koudelka exhibition at the Hayward Gallery, London, in 1984. Superb exhibits, but not hung with any consideration for effective communication with the visitor.**

Within all these broad types of exhibition circumstances, there are some important categories mostly associated with practical considerations.

TRAVELLING EXHIBITIONS

These are exhibitions which actually travel, with wheels or keels: caravans, vans, trains, ships. Even a fishing boat has been used by the Canadians. Its holds were exhibition space, and the boat itself was an exhibit quite capable of crossing the Atlantic, which

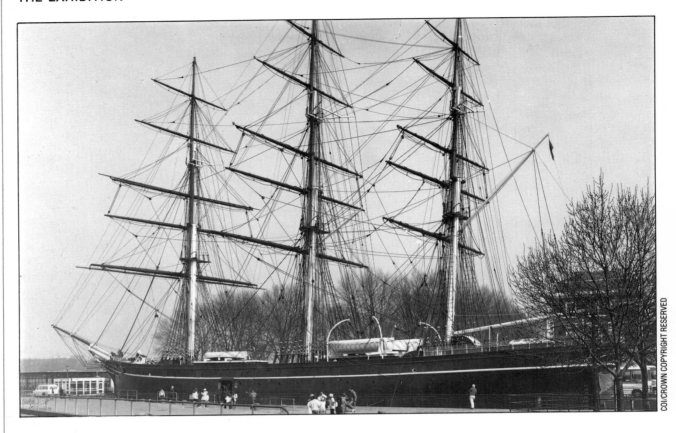

▲ The *Cutty Sark*, in dry dock at Greenwich, London, contains an exhibition about its life and times, and is itself an exhibit.

it actually did. The *Cutty Sark* is another of many examples of ships, but it does not travel, nor indeed does HMS *Belfast*. Exhibition trains have been used by both governments and private industry. The constraints are evident; they are only used as exhibitions when they are stationary. The same goes for caravans. They are normally pulled by a 'tug', often a Land Rover, which also carries a generator to supply power where there is no access to mains. Again, the constraints are obvious but it is amazing how much information can be condensed into the close viewing conditions of a train or caravan section. One most important factor is maintenance, the subject of Chapter 9, but, clearly, for a travelling exhibition it is a peculiar problem, generally demanding a permanent driver/maintenance staff.

Another difficulty is siting. With a train, ship or caravan suitable venues must be found and arranged well in advance, for it is no good embarking on a travelling show until a schedule of sites and visits has been arranged.

PORTABLE EXHIBITIONS

These of course do travel as well, but only to be erected and dismantled again and again. There are many manufactured systems available for building temporary exhibitions, most of which are exactly suitable for such treatment. They also generally come in specially designed boxes or crates, so to adapt a design to suit

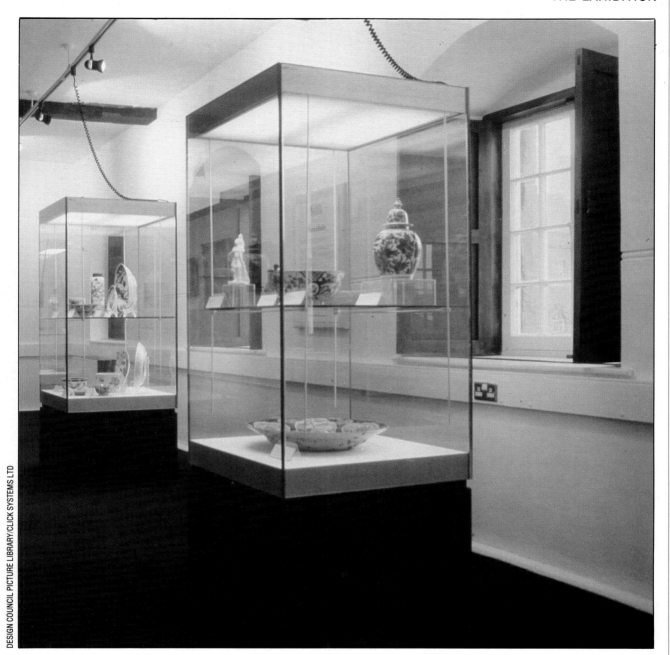

DESIGN COUNCIL PICTURE LIBRARY/CLICK SYSTEMS LTD

them makes a great deal of sense. Exhibition systems will be dealt with at greater length in Chapter 7, but of course they are not the only solution. It is often essential or beneficial to design one's own portable exhibition. Important considerations are weight, size, packaging, precious objects, ease of erection, durability in the hands of many different users and clear instructions. Also, of course, exhibitions with a working, moving or audio-visual content must be carefully considered and rejected if maintenance and power cannot be guaranteed.

▲ **A showcase construction system, Inca, by Click Systems Ltd.**

There are many other types of exhibition: conferences, hotel or station foyers, special 'one-off' exhibitions like the Festival of Britain in 1951 or Ulster '71, and the 1984 Garden Festival in Liverpool and its offspring. There are 'information-only' exhibitions, set up by government bodies or research stations at trade fairs, to explain laws or policies associated with the trade in question, or government-financed services available to the exhibitors. There are open days such as those at the Road Research Laboratory, or the Building Research Station; exhibitions in libraries or learned societies; exhibitions that verge on Disney World like Jorvik, the Viking exhibition in York — where electric cars

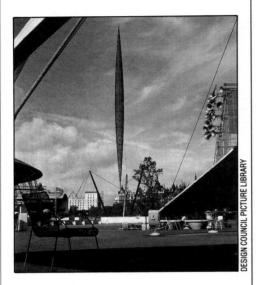

DESIGN COUNCIL PICTURE LIBRARY

▲ The 'Skylon' central feature of the Festival of Britain in 1951.

▶ Disney World, Florida. It may seem corny here but people can play a very valuable role, even in informative displays.

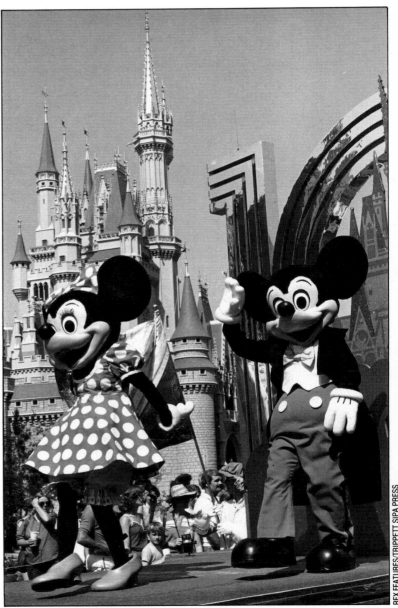

REX FEATURES/TRIPPETT SIPA PRESS

▼ Part of Jorvik, York. Static models here but real people or animated models can and have been used in other exhibitions.

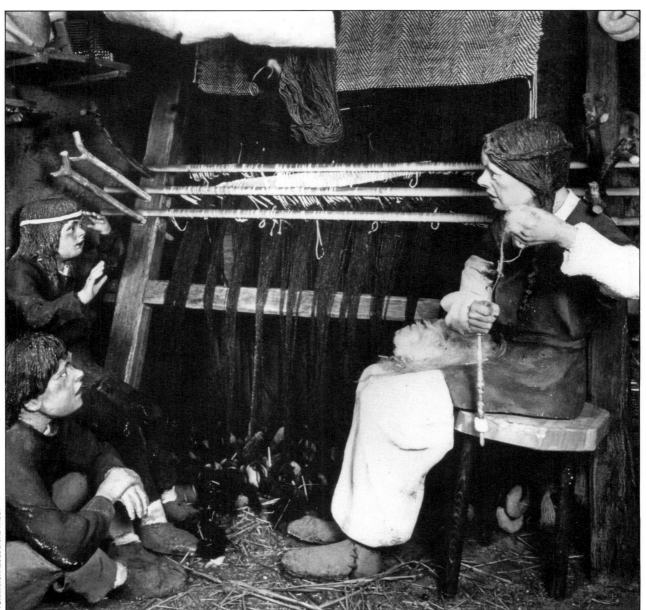

THE EXHIBITION

▼ Part of the National Motor Museum, Beaulieu, Hampshire. No real effort to display stylishly has been made here, probably because the objects are such powerful attractions in their own right.

take the visitors around the exhibition at a controlled pace, or the National Motor Museum at Beaulieu in the New Forest. There are completely new museums, such as the Museum of the Moving Image on the South Bank, devoted to one comparatively modern industry: film and television. Zoos are becoming interpretative exhibitions.

All these should involve exhibition design, as they are all dealing with objects and information in space as areas of learning and enlightenment.

——————————— NOTE ———————————

[1] International Bureau of Exhibitions (BIE), 56 Avenue Victor Hugo, 75783 Paris, Cedex 16, France.

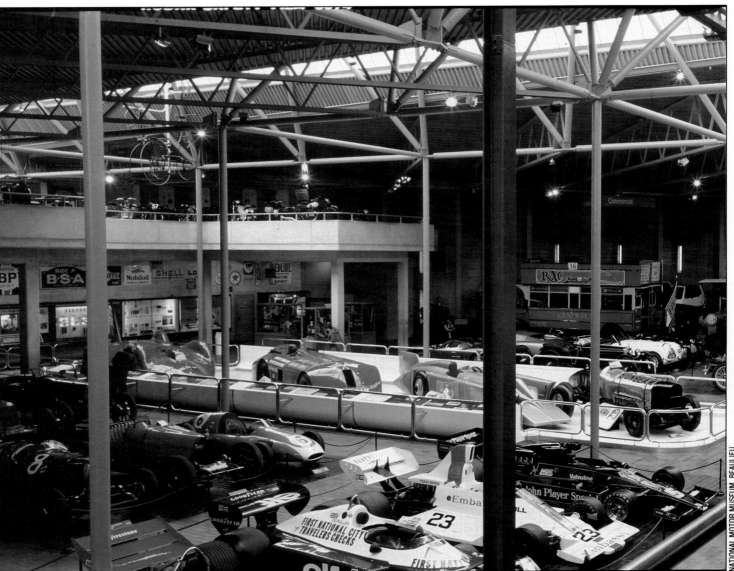

NATIONAL MOTOR MUSEUM, BEAULIEU

▼ A designer's visual of part of the
Museum of the Moving Image,
London, opened in 1988 behind the
National Film Theatre.

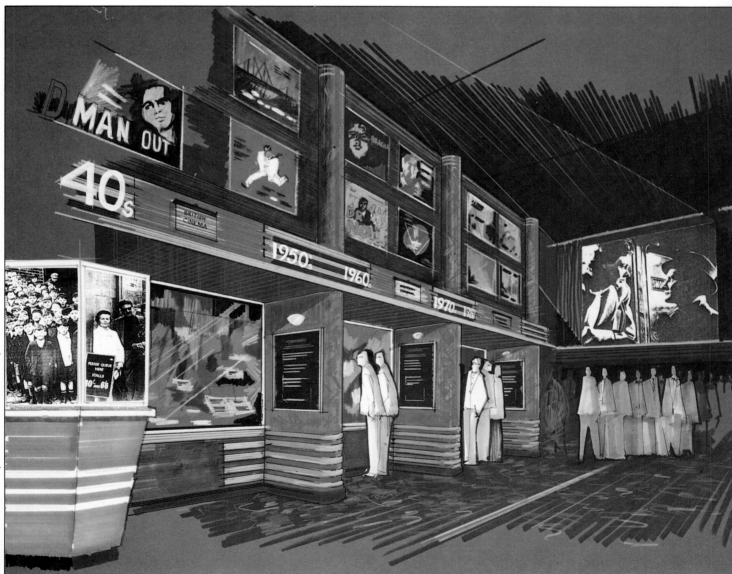

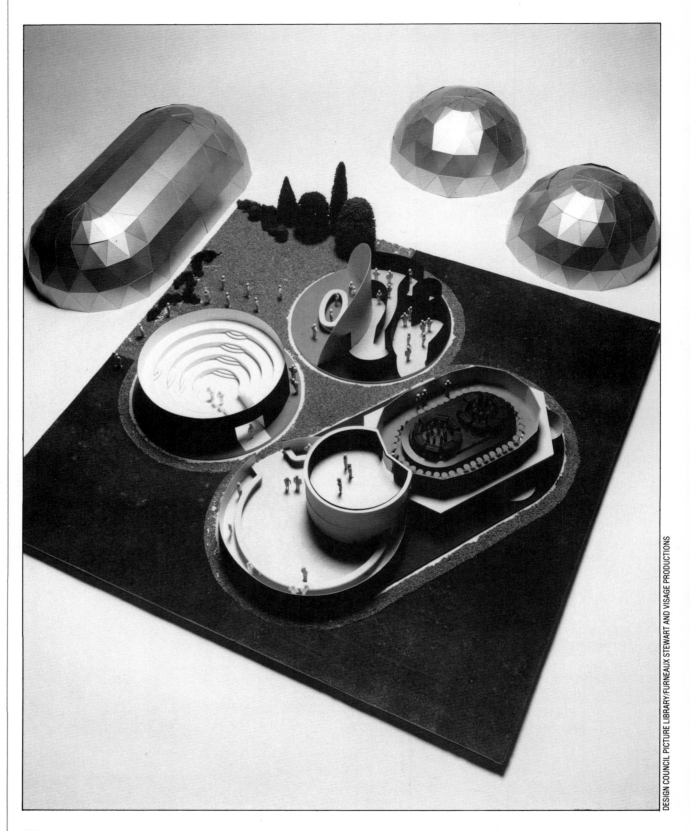

2
THE DESIGNER

Designers, like exhibitions, come in all shapes and sizes. 'Designer' is itself an odd word. Unlike the term architect, which always denotes a designer of buildings, the term designer has always to be qualified — in this case with the word 'exhibition' — and we have already seen that a great number of people are not sure what an exhibition is. This is probably why, in the early 1960s, when art colleges shook themselves out of the complacent and class-conscious distinction between fine art and commercial art, into the multidisciplinary establishments they are now, exhibition design was left out. In the smaller, diploma-oriented colleges, display courses proliferated; but even at the time of writing there is no such thing as a course offering an honours degree in exhibition design.

Where do exhibition designers come from? In the writer's own early experience, they were mostly 'lapsed' architects. However, the first designer really to earn a reputation for exhibitions was James Gardner, and his background is certainly not architectural. Gardner first came to public attention with 'Britain Can Make It' in 1946, but a leading involvement with the Festival of Britain in 1951 put him firmly on the exhibition map, along with other designers like Misha Black, and architects such as Casson, Spence and Braven. Today's generation of exhibition designers comes second-hand, as it were, generally via graphics or interiors. Neither is adequate. The former deals with flat presentation of information and the latter with people and space. Even in colleges which have fine reputations in both fields, it is commonplace for the two courses to be totally separated when it comes to projects concerning exhibitions; whereas, as will be seen, it would be an ideal area in which to develop interdisciplinary skills and group or team activity. The truth of the matter is that a feel for, and an almost sculptural comprehension of, space is essential to the exhibition designer, as is a feel for graphics and the flat presentation of information. It is quite possible for graphics or interiors students to develop the understanding required.

Ideally, exhibition design — across the wide range from trade fairs to museums — should be taught to degree level as a discipline in its own right. Selling is such a vital function in the western economy that the need for this should be evident. Since 1970 museums have become an integral part of our educational system and, just as there are no unqualified teachers, museum exhibition designers should be equally well trained. While there is no degree course, it might be hoped that there was a postgradu-

◄ Presentation models by Furneaux Stewart for the 'Fit for Life' touring exhibition, 1988. Models are powerful alternatives to visuals, but sometimes *too* powerful if the client discovers that the eventual product is not exactly like the original proposal.

ate course for suitable graphic or interior design students. There is not. It is interesting that the standards of design in museums should be currently so high, for they have actually fallen in commercial ventures, which seem to have declined since their heyday in the 1960s.

Meanwhile, a swift glance over the profession as it stands today shows practitioners coming from all fields of design or, in the author's case, none at all. This is only a bad thing if the design work is done not by a regular practitioner, but — as happens so often — by someone wholly ignorant of it, when it is possibly delegated by senior partners in design firms to junior assistants as 'a bit of fun'. Of course, exhibition design is a serious business; the fact that fun can be had from it simply demonstrates the enormous variety of skills that are needed. Despite the need for specific exhibition design training, it is also true that the exhibition designer is a jack of all trades. So many factors go into making exhibitions at their best that, without the broadest possible knowledge of methods of presenting information, the designer can be lost for solutions to some of the complex communication problems that emerge.

What qualities are needed to create the creature? They come in two categories: first, personal qualities and second, professional qualities; those that result from training or experience.

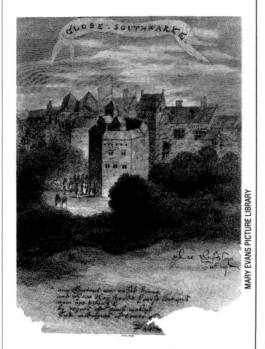

PERSONAL QUALITIES

Understanding three-dimensional space This means the ability to think in the round, to see a flat plan and to be able to project it mentally outwards into three dimensions; to be able to explore spaces in the mind; to place objects in space and to walk around or through them. Training in sculpture, interior design and architecture helps to develop these facilities.

Understanding people The designer needs to have a sensitivity to people and how they behave, interact or respond to various physical circumstances; how they enter a room, how they react to artefacts, diagrams, photographs and even each other. Every designer should be at least in part a psychologist, and in the peculiarly intimate relationship between displays and people, it is essential.

Understanding structure While it is not essential to have a degree or diploma in engineering or structural design, a certain amount of common sense about it is vital. When necessary, structural expertise can be easily brought in, but it is important in the early planning stages to know that ceilings do not generally float in space unaided; floors actually have to support enormous loads and walls will fall down if they are not propped up. Moreover, most inanimate things on legs will fall over sideways if they are not stiffly braced. This is all pretty basic information, but amazingly silly proposals have been rejected by the organisers of exhibitions and their experts.

Theatrical flair Exhibition design is considered by many to be very close to theatre. Clearly in a theatre the audience is static, and captive, and the basic reason for theatre is entertainment. However, more and more exhibitions are being built with entertainment in mind (Jorvik and Beaulieu, in the United Kingdom, for example; the Powerhouse in Sydney, and the Exploratorium in San Francisco). Many recent plays have been written with the accent on information, as indeed was much of Shakespeare and before him the Mystery Plays. A sense of theatre is a valuable attribute for the successful exhibition designer; the ability also to see the drama in a subject and to exploit it to attract a bigger audience, or explain complex ideas in an enthralling manner.

▼ **Is this a play or an exhibition? Real artefacts, true story, real actors! 'Mary After the Queen', by the Royal Shakespeare Company, Stratford-upon-Avon.**

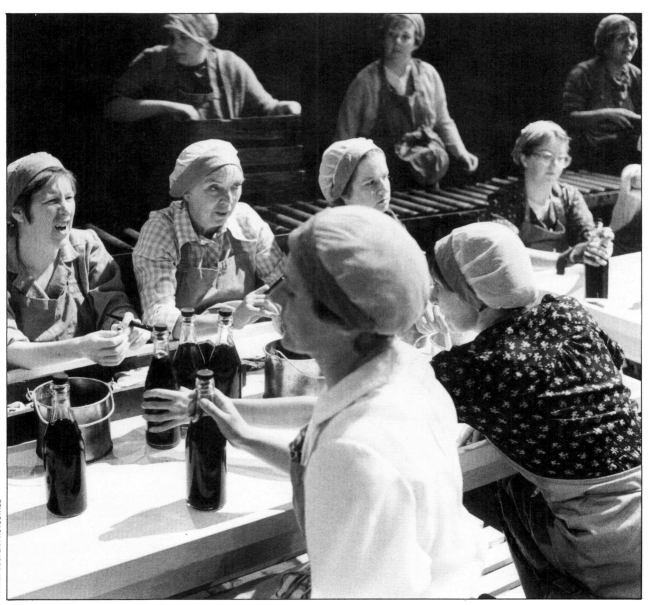

DONALD COOPER/PHOTOSTAGE

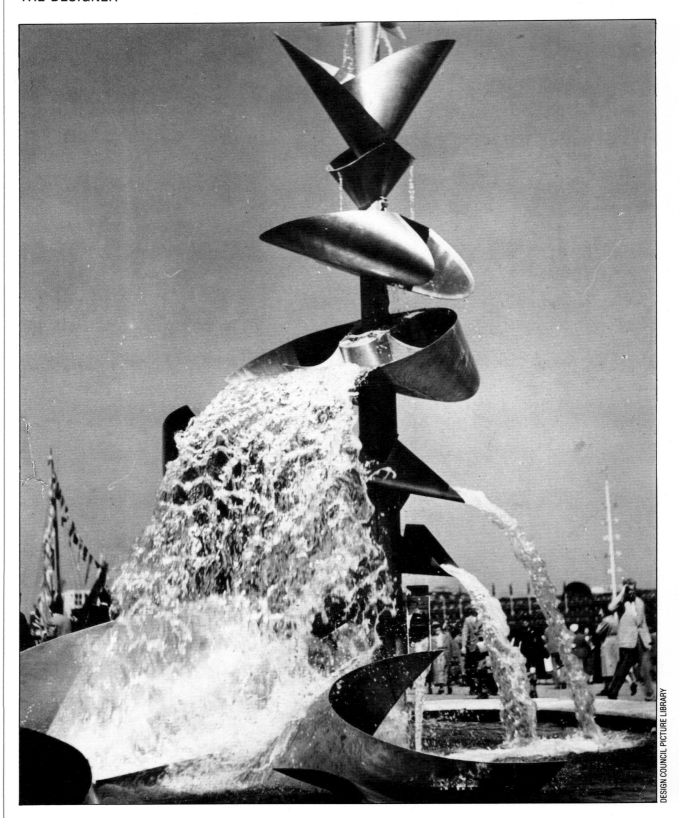

Solving problems Others, particularly Edward de Bono, have written on the subject of lateral thinking. As far as this book is concerned, it is the ability to open the mind to all kinds of solutions to design problems unconstrained by conventional attitudes. Take, for example, film projection. Films are projected on to screens — is it just that simple? Practically everything can be projected on to: smoke, spray, gauze, water, milk, people, floors, leaves. That is lateral thinking, and of course it can be applied to countless other circumstances. The ability to solve problems by this expansion of thinking is invaluable.

Intelligent interest There are two classic areas where it is most difficult to design effectively and objectively. The first is where the designer is not interested in the subject, and the second is when he is too interested, or even a specialist. In the first instance it is obvious that if the designer is not interested, he is going to find it very hard to persuade anyone else to take an interest. In the second instance, if he is a near-specialist he will fail to communicate objectively, or interpret the subject in a jargon-free manner. An intelligent interest is naturally essential. An exhibition designer should be the sort of person who is well informed, well read and able to take a short-term intense interest in any subject. In this way he or she can act as an effective interpreter, guiding the specialist suppliers of the information towards a comprehensible presentation. If they can explain it effectively to the designer, it is likely that this explanation will be understood by the visitor. This leads naturally to an interest in communication and interpretation.

Communicating It helps if the exhibition designer is literate and wants to communicate. There is a body of opinion which thinks that the best exhibition designer is an extrovert 'exhibitionist', not just having an interest in communication but needing to communicate, almost to show off. Perhaps the body is right; there is certainly very little point in embarking on a career in exhibition design if you are shy, withdrawn and do not like to mix! However, the communication must be explicit, brief and effectively levelled and balanced.

Interpretation This is the word currently in use, particularly in museums, for the intermediary role of the designer between the specialist and the public. Interpretative design is essentially being able to understand the public and the subject well enough to interpret between them.

———————————— PROFESSIONAL QUALITIES ————————————

We move on to the professional training needed to make an exhibition designer. Ideally, there should be a degree course available, but, as has been pointed out, there is no such thing. Therefore somehow the student of exhibition design must acquire the following training:

◄ **Aluminium fountain outside Sea and Ships Pavilion, Festival of Britain, 1951. Water can be lovely, both visually and aurally, in an exhibition but it's a nightmare if dealt with by amateurs.**

43

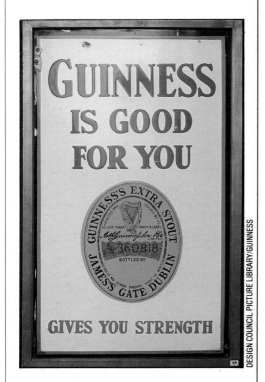

▲ An advertisement you might or might not believe.

Interior design Training in the comprehension and use of interior space, which is quite different from exterior space — an introvert understanding of it as opposed to an extrovert one. The training to place people, objects and information within a specific empty space. The comprehension of that void, its characteristics and potential, allied to a broad grounding in safety factors and the law relating to the safety of visitors with regard to fire, structure and services.

Structural engineering Naturally, any structure that will contain people, or support or house heavy or precious exhibits must be safe. Basic training in this area is vital.

Graphics It is possible to communicate without words, but they are normally an important ingredient. A later chapter is devoted to words in exhibitions, the understanding of which is fundamental training for a designer. There is no need for professional, degree standard qualifications, but the exhibition designer must appreciate the necessity for the use of a professional graphic designer in almost any successful communication exercise.

The English language Training in clear, precise writing is essential. First, for any professional the ability to communicate clearly is of enormous help in drafting reports, synopses and briefs. Second, as has already been stated, communication is what exhibitions are about and, while exhibitions of words alone are anathema, exhibitions of objects must be supported at least minimally by words. Frequently the designer will take on the role of scriptwriter for want of anyone better to perform the function.

Lighting This is a great deal less haphazard than it used to be, and actual training in lights and lighting techniques is invaluable. In museums, light can be a major problem due to its effects on fragile fabrics, artwork and dyes. Conservationists should be on hand or consulted. Meanwhile, there have been many new light fittings developed over the years and it is as well to be up to date.

Drawing board skills and drawing ability These are obvious practical necessities. Drawing and sketching from life are marvellous ways of perceiving and understanding objects and space. Any designer will be improved by regular activity of this kind. The same is true of photography. Many photographic techniques are exploited in exhibition work. Photographs and photographic enlargements are frequently used; slides, photomontages, films and television are all photography. Such techniques are also used in the production and enlargement of text and diagrams. A basic grounding in photographic techniques is essential.

Model making Models are frequently used for presentation of designs to a client, or in the exhibition itself. An ability to make presentation models is of value, though it is a time-consuming process. This ability leads to a greater understanding of the problems involved in the making of models for display purposes by professional model makers.

Water and plumbing It is surprising how often water is used in exhibitions, sometimes as a decorative feature, fountain or cascade, or as a necessary part of an exhibit. Some idea of its quirks and peculiarities is essential, as is a healthy and wary respect for it. Water out of control is of course something to be avoided.

▼ Mural, transparencies and objects in 'The Story of the Earth', Geological Museum, 1972.

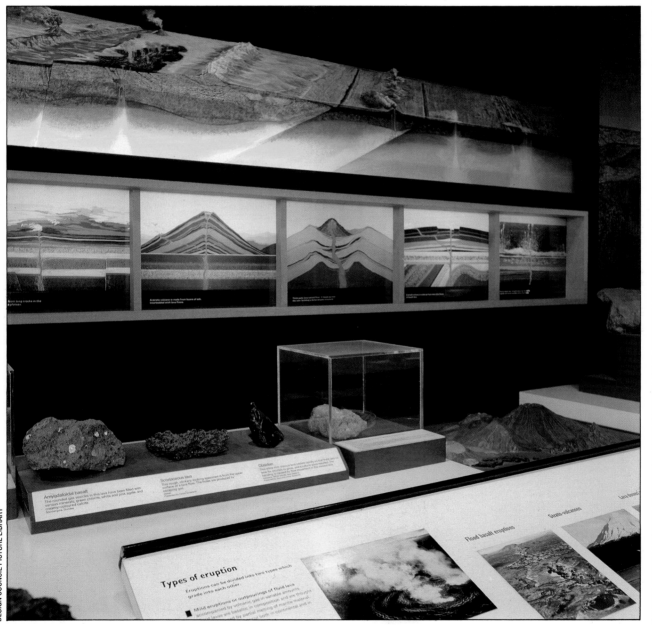

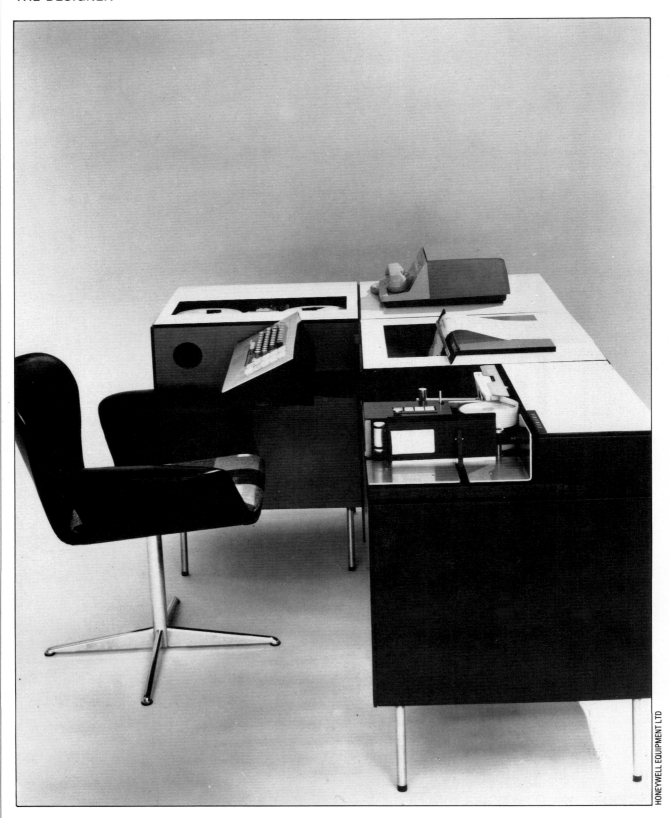

Electronics and mechanical engineering Not everybody can acquire these skills. The writer is famously ignorant with regard to anything electronic. An understanding of the potential capabilities of contemporary technology is, along with an inventive mind, of great benefit in devising the often complex three-dimensional means of communicating things simply.

Computers Clearly these now play an increasing part in all sorts of communication and design. Anything written now will be out of date almost before the pen leaves the page. An early introduction to computers is therefore vital, as is regular contact with their development.

Painting Murals and mural treatments are often used in exhibitions. It is necessary to acquire knowledge of their production, reproduction and enlargement. Professional mural artists should always be used and they can be found through their professional associations.

Illustration and diagrams Again, these are frequently used. Clearly, it is better to use professionals, as with painting, but it is important to have some training in illustrating and in generating informative diagrams out of often complex information, in order to understand the problems which can arise.

Management A whole chapter is devoted to this subject, from which it should become clear how vital good management is to good design. At best, designers should be supported by management services, but at the very least a designer should know how to manage the production of an exhibition and to control the finances involved.

Advertising This is generally associated with claims for a product. Exhibitions generally demonstrate the product itself, and that is their great value: an inbuilt integrity. When an exhibition stand is erected simply to make unsubstantiated claims, this is advertising and the writer has no expertise in the field.

All these subjects are ideals in any training, and there is no reason why they should not be part of a three-year degree course. Many people have gained their knowledge of these things by experience, and there is no harm in that. The diversity and range of subjects which make an ideal background for the exhibition designer is therefore very broad. This highlights the 'jack of all trades' aspect. However, with the right training it should be possible to be master of at least one: exhibition design.

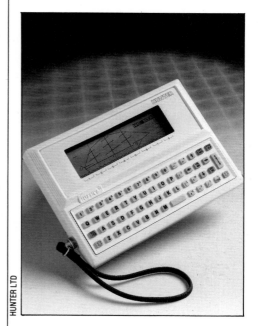

HUNTER LTD

▲ A computer, circa 1983.

◀ A computer, circa 1966.

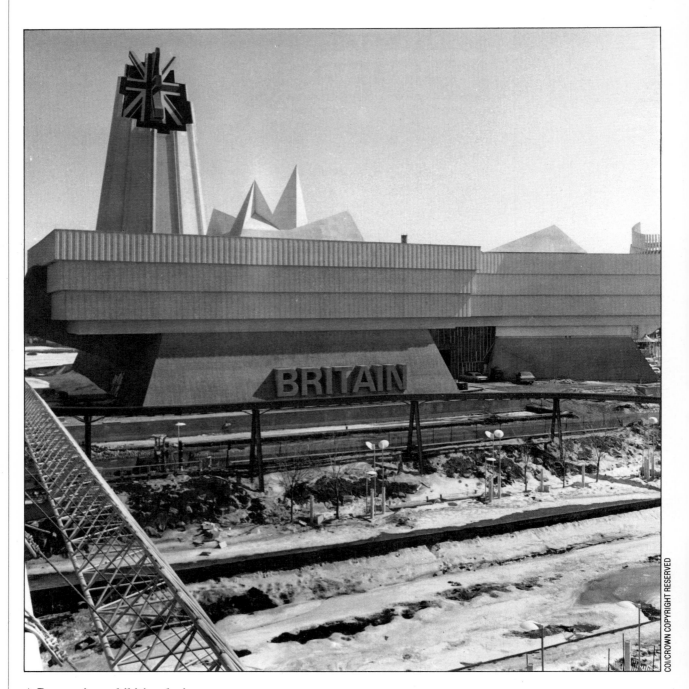

▲ Persuasive exhibition design.
The British Pavilion, Expo '67,
Montreal. Critics thought the
message a little confusing. The
disintegrating Union Jack falling
down the factory chimney, perhaps?

3
THE BRIEF

Now that it has been decided what an exhibition is and what sort of designer is required, it is possible to advance upon a project.

An exhibition is only going to be built because it has been agreed that it is the only solution to a particular problem; the best method of exposition and communication in particular circumstances. It is not possible, or better, to make a film, TV programme or commercial. An advertisement, brochure or book is not what is needed. A record will not do. An exhibition is required because there is something to exhibit and a story to be told that can best be put across in three-dimensional terms.

Six things must first be established:

— The aims and exact goals of the exhibition
— The venue and exact site
— The information in general terms
— The objects to be displayed
— The opening date
— The budget.

These six factors are basic. If any of them are changed during planning, design or construction the project will be radically affected. It is therefore vital that they are agreed between client, designer and management at the earliest possible moment and then maintained as crucial to the success of the venture.

The six prime factors can be described in more detail.

THE AIMS

Until recently the actual effects of an exhibition were either guessed at or optimistically forecast. Over the last decade, starting in America, studies have been made to elicit the precise effects of displays using psychological techniques and statistics. These methods of evaluation will be discussed in Chapter 10 but, clearly, some knowledge of the effect of various types of display is of great value when deciding what one is aiming to achieve. Like all professional expertise, evaluation has to be paid for. This kind of information can affect radically the success or failure of either a commercial or public exhibition; so if there is an insufficient body of experience to help decide the aims, this is probably worth buying in.

These aims can be summarised in the following set of objectives. To sell, not often in the sense of directly selling an object,

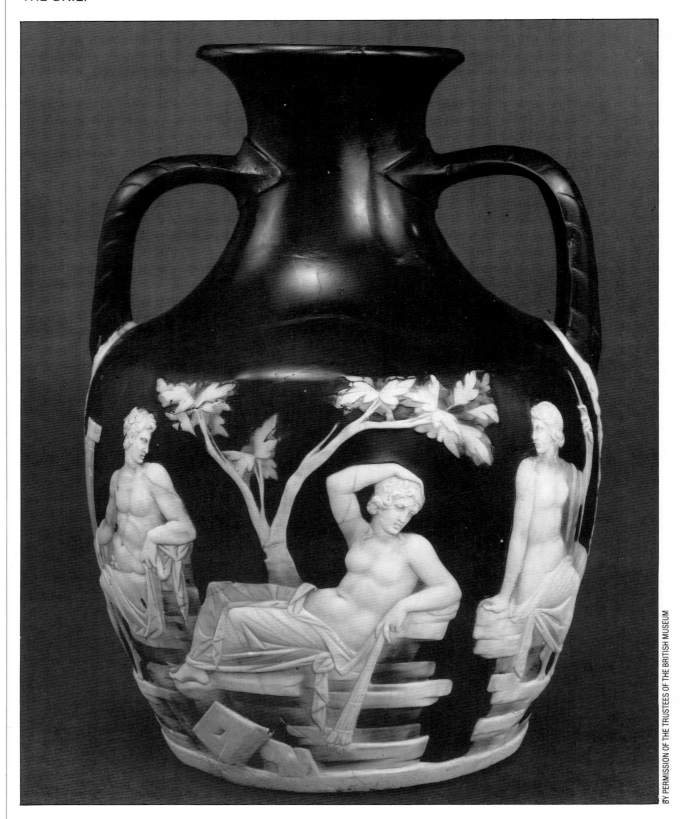

but to sell in the abstract — showing an object off for close scrutiny and even handling, so that a client may be persuaded to buy in bulk; supplying a piece of equipment; selling an invention. To persuade in the sense of pressuring the public; convincing the visitor that, for instance, 'Britain is Best' or that dealing with agriculture or the environment is best done this way or that. Persuading encompasses respecting the countryside, visiting a certain town, holding a conference here or there, using certain services, voting for a certain party, supporting a cause or visiting a museum. To expose by putting a collection on display, giving the public a sight of rare artefacts or masterpieces, getting public reaction to a prototype or architectural scheme. To parade a new acquisition or gift; to be seen. To inform by describing a new product or concept, keeping the public up to date with commercial, political or social developments. To explain new or ancient aspects of science, technology or research and make clear any services available. To advise the public about their rights and the law. Finally to generate interest in a subject by developing it thematically or systematically. To delight, and why not? The exhibition can be there simply in order to give pleasure, to entertain or perhaps to allow people an opportunity to see something rare or special. To enlighten — a mixture of the last four and what exhibitions are really all about. One dictionary definition of enlightenment is 'to become wiser through knowledge', and the exhibition is a unique vehicle for that.

THE SITE

Without information about the specific site within the venue, it is impossible to design. Working in a vacuum is not possible for a designer, though he can introduce ideas about design philosophy, methods and treatments. Until the site is decided, nothing concrete can emerge. Where is the venue? Variations can be astonishing, and great fun — from a barn in the middle of a river delta (the Musée Camarguais) to a car park under a road bridge in central London (the Museum of the Moving Image); from a library in Thurso, Scotland, to a sophisticated, purpose-built complex in Frankfurt. There is no limit to where an exhibition can be, as long as both the exhibitor and the public can reach it relatively easily. The best venue, either on or off the beaten track, has good public transport, parking, restaurant, toilet and power facilities, but some very successful exhibitions make do with a good deal less. Many a 'one-off' show does not fit into the normal run of exhibitions and therefore cannot be included in a trade fair, for instance, at a specifically designed exhibition complex. Special situations are needed for these — and so is lateral thinking. What is actually required is a clean, generally covered space with easy access to power — usually electricity. Examples are station forecourts, hotel foyers, underground or overground car parks, airport terminals, squares, parks, piazzas and city centres. The latter open areas can take tents, geodesic structures, inflatable pavilions or portable industrial sheds, most of

◀ A possession or an acquisition worth parading. The Portland Vase, one of the many treasures at the British Museum.

which are available for hire. A mobile exhibition may be under consideration; it should be situated if possible near power and easy public access, but again the possibilities are great. Trains, lorries, buses, trailers, caravans, liners, warships, fishing boats and probably even aeroplanes (were the subject apposite and the plane available). Once the decision of venue is taken, the site — the actual specific area within the venue on which the exhibition will be placed — is the next vital piece of information. Ideally, a visit should be made by the exhibitor and the designer, and a number of factors noted:

— Accessibility Access both for the visitor and the exhibitor; lifts, loading size and weight, lorry or goods access, parking, delivery, unloading and loading gear or platforms.
— The size length, width and shape of the floor and floor loading.
— Height Overhead obstructions, exposed wiring, lighting or dangerously exposed services, headroom for cranes or fork-lifts. The ceiling construction and strength; the facility for hanging signs or structures. Anything on the site like power outlets to which other exhibitors might need access.
— Daylight Is there daylight at all? Will it interfere with display lighting? Will there be awkward oblique light in the early evening? Can it be controlled, shuttered or blinded off?
— Services Electricity, gas, water, drainage, compressed air, ventilation and air conditioning, telephone — where are they all? How easy is it to get to them? What is the electricity supply, phase and voltage (AC or DC)? What is the maximum loading?
— The law pertaining to the site if there is general public access is often different if the access becomes restricted. What types of exhibits or displays may be used? Will flammable plastics, timber or fabrics be permitted? Can working exhibits be displayed? Can tall structures be built? What are the fire and safety regulations? If the designer recognises, seeks out and observes the law — which is generally designed for the good of the public — then there will be no costly and embarrassing changes to make while the exhibitor is trying to entertain his first visitor.

THE INFORMATION

At the earliest possible stage all the information to be communicated must be available, ideally as part of the brief. It does not need to have been edited into perfect exhibition form or text, but it must be there. It consists of all the ideas that need to be expressed, all the background data and statistics, hopefully everything that a sizeable percentage of the visitors will learn. If it is not possible to get all the detailed data together, many a brief has evolved with the exhibitor knowing generally what needs to be communicated, and leaning heavily on the designer for how to say it.

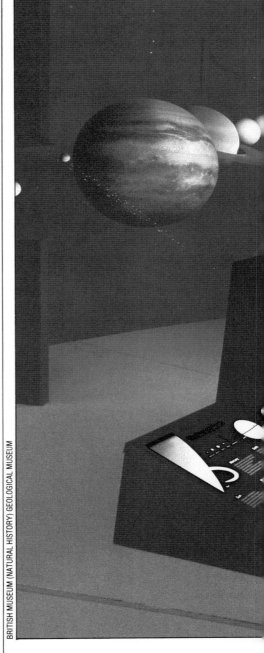

▲ To enlighten: a multi-media display, 'The Story of the Earth', Geological Museum, 1972. This was the first of its kind, dealing with geology, anywhere in the world.

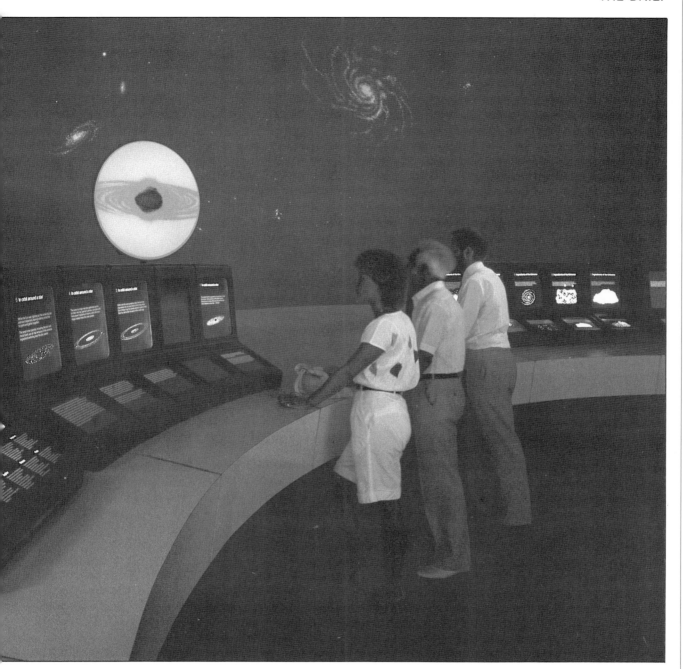

Some concepts cannot be expressed in the three-dimensional terms used at their best in an exhibition, and the designer's experience will be invaluable in making certain decisions. In organisations that employ their own designers, it is ideal for briefs to be evolved between the initiators of the information and the presenters of the information. In this way no time is wasted in going down blind alleys towards exhibitions which will prove impractical, impossible or vastly expensive. No matter what, it is difficult to start developing any exhibition until a large amount is known about the informative content. There are specialist exhibition editors or scriptwriters, and if there is a fair amount of information to be expressed, rather than just simple labels for exhibits, it is at this stage that these professionals should be brought in. Some large design practices employ such people on their staff; a few designers can and do perform this editorial role. In many national museums editors are, quite rightly, an integral part of the design team, while some large companies employ copywriters.

THE OBJECTS

Some exhibitions have no objects except those made in an effort to communicate: special models which 'diagramatically' explain subjects too complex for either words or illustrations. Ideally, however, exhibitions are about things — to see, hear, touch, smell or even taste. Sometimes they are inside the object on display: the Smokey Mountains; the *Cutty Sark*. Generally, however, they are the vehicles for displaying and certain things must be ascertained by the designer at an early stage because, of course, they will affect his or her thinking and planning.

The number and size of the exhibits is clearly important; their point loading too, for a car may weigh a tonne but the load on each of its wheels will be many tonnes per square centimetre. This is the way floor loading is measured. Are the exhibits

▶ An exhibit in the Smokey Mountains National Park, Tennessee. This house is maintained doorless and empty throughout the year.

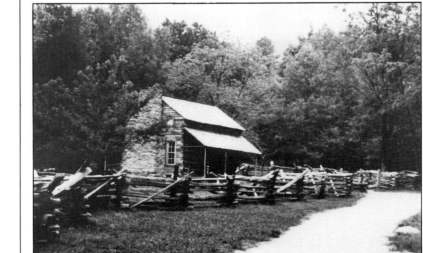

GILES VELARDE

spontaneously flammable? Fragile? Precious? Will they be sensitive to light, heat or movement? Do they need a special atmosphere or through-draught of air? Do they need a dust-free environment? Do they collect static electricity and dust? Can they be touched? If to be hung on a wall, do they require special hanging points, plinths or barriers? Do they need their own showcases or frames, or will these have to be made? They might be valuable, very valuable or priceless. However, there is no point in hiring expensive security guards before the priceless objects arrive. What are the insurance characteristics in transit or on display? Government property is rarely insured; it is covered by government indemnity which simply means that the government will replace it. This is difficult if we are talking about a Turner and easy if we are talking about a tank.

These questions are almost endless, but essential. Other considerations are security, supervision, freighting across borders and through customs, and delivery addresses. A good manager will take care of the details, but most of these facts must be known by the designer at an early stage, because they will either affect the design or affect things which could delay or confuse completion and construction.

When all the exhibits have been decided and all their characteristics known, the designer might make card shapes or models to scale to represent them, and displace them about the site or showcase. Whatever the choice, they must be designed 'in' and not simply left to be 'artistic arrangements' made when they arrive the day before the exhibition opens. This is not a good time to make creative decisions. The designer should be involved in the selection of exhibits where there is a choice, and should see and measure them before they become 'lost' in the lengthy process of packing and shipping. Photographs can help the designer if there is no access to the exhibits and even, as an *aide-mémoire*, if there is. It is poor practice when the designer is forced to produce a design based on only a skimpy knowledge of the objects to be displayed, and an exhibitor who does not provide maximum access to this information cannot blame the designer for a poor display on opening day.

THE OPENING DATE

This is another vital bit of information required in the brief. It is not actually essential to know the exact day, but it is a good idea to commit all involved to a date at the earliest possible stage. This is particularly important when VIPs are to be invited to open the exhibition. Most trade fairs have a set opening date, determined by the complex calendar for the exhibition hall. These dates have to take into account the building and dismantling times which vary, for instance, between the pre-constructed booth exhibitions of the USA and the Motor Show where huge and complicated stands need perhaps ten days on site to build. An exhibition in a museum or gallery may be tied to an anniversary or a gap in the museum's programme of events.

The suitability of a date must be considered. A flower show in mid-winter might hit a snag or two, but some dates have problems which are not so obvious. It is possible to arrange an opening date which coincides with a local football match. Beware, too, of special feast-days or anniversaries. Before deciding a date, it is as well to consult the local council and police to be sure it does not conflict. If it is to be a grand occasion, royalty needs at least six months' advance notice, and sometimes a year. Some dates are bad for other reasons. Most people write off the season over Christmas and the New Year; ten days are generally lost, so it is fine to open an exhibition early in the New Year as long as an extra fortnight is allowed for preparation. The same is true of summer holidays and, to some extent, Easter. All this applies to western countries only and the Middle and Far East have a different set of constraints.

Some days are better than others. Tuesday is a good day — the preceding weekend can be used to cram in extra work and Monday to purchase anything discovered missing on Sunday. But again, these characteristics vary from country to country. Friday is a bad day in the UK. People are prone to want to go home, 'exhausted' by their week's work, so it is difficult to get visitors for an opening celebration in the afternoon. Perhaps it is better in the morning!

▼ No matter their other charms, Royalty do galvanise activity to meeting opening dates, and frequently provide the impetus for improving the facilities in an old museum or exhibition hall.

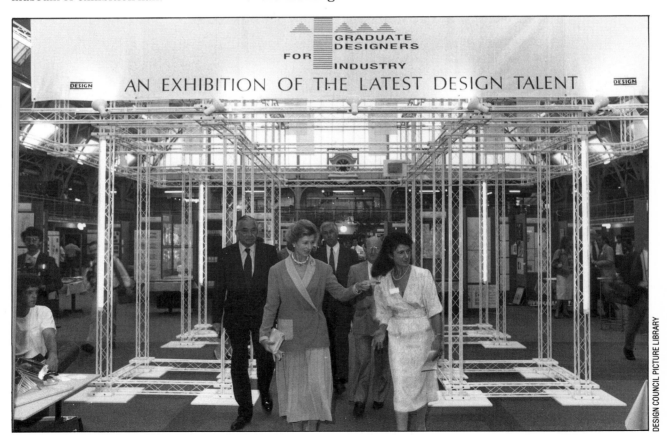

DESIGN COUNCIL PICTURE LIBRARY

The press must be allowed early access, if you invite them at all, so that an article with a photograph can be produced on opening day. Rumour has it that the press will not come unless there is plenty of drink about, and the phrase 'cordially invited' is supposed to imply that there will be.

So, opening dates have to be picked early and carefully, and not changed. It is useful to have a common goal; besides, if royalty is invited the date really is fixed. A royal visit not only provides an air of excitement, but a stimulus to local councils and ministries to rectify local omissions such as bad pavements outside halls or museums, or bad toilet facilities inside state- or council-owned premises to be visited.

However, not everything can be catered for, and natural disasters, assassinations or wars have been known to leave carefully planned openings looking like the Stock Exchange on a Sunday.

THE BUDGET

The final essential piece of information. A proper budget can only be allocated with experience and any costing quoted here would date rapidly and vary from country to country. The best way of allocating monies is by the square metre or square foot (the former is almost exactly ten times the latter). These measurements refer to a square metre 'super', that is from the floor of the site to the top of the exhibition structure. They refer also to the whole area of the exhibition, public, staff and display space. Obviously a square metre of aisle will cost a great deal less than a square metre of complex three-dimensional display, but an overall costing will serve as a good guide.

Early guesstimating can only be done with experience, but there are a number of known factors that can be ascertained: hire of exhibition space, site rental, square foot cost of photographic reproduction, character cost of typesetting, the making of certain special models, hire of furniture, designers' fees and so on. Any established designer or exhibition manager should be able to quote approximate costs per square metre for the specific types of exhibitions described in Chapter 1. Experienced exhibition designers can be found in the UK through the Chartered Society of Designers, and experienced managers, in government agencies such as the Central Office of Information or the Design Council, will usually help with advice.

The cost is an integral part of the design brief. It is fundamental. Designers who exceed their budget by more than 10 per cent (a safe contingency to allow for seasonal price fluctuations etc) is as guilty of bad practice as one who designs an exhibition the wrong way round.

With these six vital statistics established and agreed in writing, it is possible to embark upon the project confidently without the fear that radical changes will be made which might confuse or affect the design to the detriment of the finished product.

THE Sun

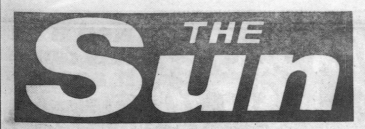

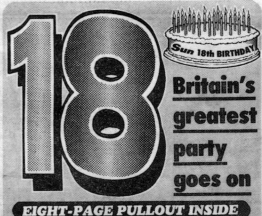

18

Sun 18th BIRTHDAY

Britain's greatest party goes on

EIGHT-PAGE PULLOUT INSIDE

Wednesday, November 18, 1987   20p   **TODAY'S TV IS ON PAGE 14**

£30,000 TRINGO BINGO

Today's numbers are on Page 13

Ronald Reagan . . . new crisis

Outlaw! Reagan rocked by Iran report

SUN FOREIGN DESK

PRESIDENT Reagan was plunged into a new crisis last night as Irangate investigators accused him of violating the U.S. Constitution.

He was blasted by 18 members of the 26-strong Congressional committee that probed the illegal supply of arms to Contra rebels in Nicaragua.

Their report says Reagan failed in his constitutional duty to "take care that the laws be faithfully executed."

The President has always maintained that he knew nothing of the Contra plan until after it actually happened.

But according to BBC sources in Washington, the committee was deeply suspicious of his claim.

And the report says that even if Reagan did **NOT** know about the diversion of American money to the rebels, he **SHOULD** have done.

The report—compiled on the direction of Congress's majority Democrats—also accuses the

Continued on Page Two

BLONDE WEDS 7 SOLDIERS IN 16 YEARS

(not to mention a sailor)

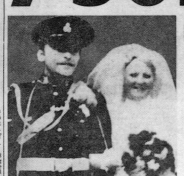

Groom No 8 . . . Patricia and lance-corporal Ken

BLONDE Patricia Jackson was behind bars last night after marrying seven soldiers and a sailor in 16 years—four of them bigamously.

The story of the khaki-crazy nurse's marriage-go-round was revealed when she was jailed for six months for bigamy. Patricia, 34, married soldier No 1 in 1971 and a string of husbands—legal and illegal—followed.

The latest in line was Lance Corporal Kenneth Edwards, whom she "married" last year when he was home on leave from the Germany-based Staffordshire Regiment. The couple lived in married quarters for only eight weeks before Patricia was arrested for bigamy.

Kenneth, 30, was stunned to hear his "wife" had been held as she stepped off a Channel ferry on a trip back to Britain.

He had not realised she was already married to a Merchant Navy officer.

And he did not know she was on the run from jail, where she had been serving three years for deception.

Former neighbours of Patricia in Colchester, Essex, told last night of her obsession with men in uniform.

Divorcee Pat Scott said:

By KIERON SAUNDERS

"I fixed her up with work in a local pub. She claimed she knew all about cocktails.

"But she couldn't even pull a pint. The only thing she was good at pulling was soldiers.

NERVE

"She once stayed with me, but I had to kick her out—she was turning my home into a knocking shop.

"She had more boyfriends in the three weeks she was here than most women have in ten years.

"I don't know what they saw in her—she was blonde but she had black teeth."

Kenneth's mum Kath

Continued on Page Two

DIRK PARALYSED

VETERAN actor Dirk Bogarde has been left paralysed down one side by a stroke, it was revealed last night.

The 66-year-old star is in London's exclusive King Edward VII Hospital—where his close companion Tony Forward is keeping a bedside vigil.

By RUKI SAYID

Bogarde's condition is "fair" and doctors are waiting to see if the paralysis will be permanent.

The actor, who had been putting the finishing touches to his film The Vision, was taken ill

at his Chelsea home.

His agent Theo Cowan said: "It's a shock. I didn't realise there was anything wrong."

Bogarde, British matinee idol of the 1950s, went on to star in Doctor In The House, The Servant and many other hit films.

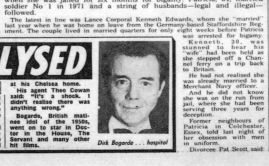

Dirk Bogarde . . . hospital

4
THE WORDS

One might expect in a book about design that when words are mentioned, it is the look of them — their typography, layout and display — that will be talked about. Quite right; but not only the look. In order for words to be effective in the 'walk-about' context of exhibitions, it goes without saying that they should be well displayed, but for that to happen they should actually be written with display in mind.

Interpretation is the word increasingly used in the context of museum exhibitions and environment centres. It means the interpretation of artefacts, works of art and science for the layperson, along with the landscape or local archaeology. In these areas the designer can play an important role. He or she is a layperson when it comes to actual academic study of the sciences involved. The designer's position between the academic source of information and the visitor is of immense value, provided that integrity as a non-specialist is maintained. The moment the designer becomes a fan, a devotee or an amateur 'student', his or her value begins to be lost. As a skilled amateur student, the scientific jargon would become second nature, coupled with an inability to differentiate between the technical language of the academic and the jargon-free explanation with which the interested layperson can understand relevant details.

A primary, interpretative role, as with language interpreters, should be performed by someone who is fluent in both technical and exhibition languages. The secondary role is more subtle. Before an exhibition can be embarked upon, the designer must know and understand what it is about. To this end the specialist, whether environmentalist, archaeologist, art historian or engineer, must explain the subject and theme satisfactorily to the designer. This process will undoubtedly involve the use of words and expressions the designer does not understand. In the further explanation of these phrases, an easily comprehended version is likely to emerge. If the designer can understand it, so will the visitor. The latter, however, is not a single unified creature of median intelligence; so hierarchies have to be introduced wherein each person can find a level of understanding and so gain something from the information imparted.

It is vital in the academic/designer interchanges for notes to be taken, for academics who are trained to communicate clearly with other academics can frequently communicate orally far more simply and effectively face to face with an interested lay inquisitor. This secondary interpretative role of the designer is much

◀ Is this designed for short-sighted readers?

under-rated but can, under sympathetic circumstances, eliminate the need for an actual interpreter or editor on a production team.

The arch-exponents of words for simple, eye-catching display are the popular newspapers. The editor does not put SEX–DRUGS–WAR in huge print at the top of page one because the readers are short-sighted; those words are there to be seen from miles away so that the person without the newspaper will buy one, the editor having surmised that those words will attract readers. It is the choice of the headlines that is a vital part of the sale of newspapers. The editor can do (and generally does) whatever he wants after that. In very crude terms, this sums up writing for exhibitions. Without giving — or being able to give — a dissertation on writing English, it is necessary to dwell for a while upon writing for exhibitions.

THE STORY

This must primarily be a story suitable for an exhibition. It must be strongly visual and factual, for concepts, theories and philosophies do not translate easily into three-dimensional presentations. It must be able to be broken down into short aspects, chapters or statements and it must itself be short. Concentrating on long narratives is difficult in the normal standing position of the visitor. Preceding the ideal story must be a title; this too must be short because it has to be put up in big print and seen from long distances. This is one of the reasons why companies with long names give themselves distinctive, initials-only, logos. The company name is often the first thing to be seen of a commercial exhibition. Special exhibitions in museums or galleries for instance need pithy, easy to say (and remember) titles, and must be graphically satisfactory. Quotation marks, apostrophes and hyphens are untidy in the often huge scale of fascias. Some groups of letters, especially upper and lower case together, can create an ugly or even subliminally suggestive shape which is best avoided.

Headings

Assuming that the story can be broken up, the next things to be considered are the titles to these divisions: the headings. These comprise the guide to the lateral subdivisions of the story — and lateral is the word. Information in exhibitions is transmitted and received laterally; the visitor moves around on the horizontal plane. The story is presented on panels or in areas of explanatory text and pictures, or in areas or rooms within the overall, informative, space. Again, the headings should be short and easily comprehended. They must also serve as a lateral guide and, when read consecutively, present a synopsis of the subject.

Hierarchies

Mention of headings, and even sub-headings, leads naturally to a discussion of hierarchies. Headings are frequently the first level in a two- or three-tier hierarchy of information. Hierarchies are

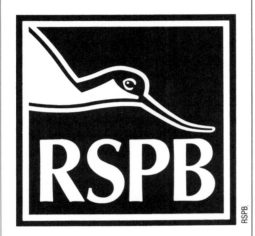

RSPB

▲ An easily seen and remembered logo.

used to enable visitors to dip — with a facility peculiar to exhibitions — into whatever part of the exhibition that interests them. Thus, standing perhaps at the entrance of an exhibition boldly entitled ENGLISH CHEESE, visitors from Somerset can read at a glance a summary of everything immediately relevant and then, by a simple turn of the head, can select the section on CHEDDAR, a particular interest. They can then make straight for it, passing Cheshire, Stilton, Wensleydale *et al.* on the way, and, on arrival at Cheddar, will perhaps be confronted by a vertical hierarchy. This is a displacement of information in short paragraphs, pictures and examples which can be 'read' downwards to the point where interest expires or technical jargon overtakes the visitors' knowledge. If interest increases with the information being learned, they might be encouraged to move in closer to more detailed displays, so that a mass of hitherto concealed information becomes apparent. Visitors at the lowest, deepest level of the hierarchy might almost be termed as 'studying', but they are doing this of their own volition.

If thoughtfully designed, the finer levels of the hierarchy would be invisible to any visitor approaching the chosen section, only becoming apparent on delving deeper and deeper into the subject. This is because another, less motivated visitor might be put off, for example, from going into the Cheddar area at all if a mass of complex and detailed information is immediately evident. Obviously, if this vertical local narrative is written in an unbroken way, then it will be difficult to display and therefore read in the way described above; so it must be written in short sentences and paragraphs, starting, for instance, with the most remarkable or illustratable characteristics. This clearly requires experience of exhibitions, but if successfully done, the exhibition and graphic designers will be able to proceed with presentation without having to ask the initiators of the information to rewrite large chunks to suit display techniques.

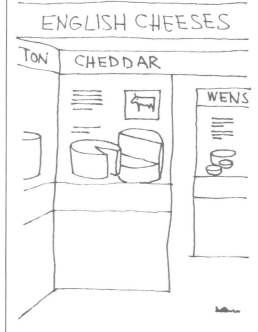

One-level exhibitions are of course another completely acceptable alternative. Here the producers select a level of intelligence and write all the text with that specific group in mind. There are varying types of IQ: reading, creative and mathematical, for instance, and there are clear differences between the reading ages of 'popular' and 'quality' press readers. Data is available, but in the UK the reading ages vary from between 9 and 17. If, for example, an age group of between 14 and 16 is selected, then it is likely that the content will be easily understood by quite a wide audience; most people in the West attempt at least to reach that scholastic level. There are two main disadvantages to this one-level approach. The first is that these academic levels are only theoretical and thus inexact, and the second is that one level excludes two distinct groups — those well below (young children) and those well above (serious students of the subject or amateur specialists). The hierarchic system at best caters for all, but it demands a great deal more from the producers, writers and designers and is therefore unpopular with organisations which want a quick production line for permanent exhibitions or a large number of popular temporaries.

Style

Another aspect of exhibition writing which applies right across the board is more concerned with the descriptive style. Colourful, subjectively descriptive prose is both useless and offensive when the object is there on display. Captions describing, 'this beautiful painting . . .' or 'this elegant dress . . .' are simply irritating. The visitor, confronted by the objects, should make an independent decision about beauty or elegance. In effect, the exhibition itself is a superlative factor. The object will certainly not be on display if it is one of several million, or a banal example, unless of course its popularity and ordinariness are the interesting factors. The exhibition must tacitly provide the adjectives and adverbs — all the visitor needs are objects and facts.

Labels and Captions

Facts lead us clearly into the area of labels and captions. For the sake of this work, a label contains the vital statistics of the object on display and the caption is a small piece of text, linking the

▼ **The Clore Gallery, London, designed by James Stirling, 1987. Unbelievable relationship between object and caption, the viewing distance for the former being probably four metres, and the latter just over one metre.**

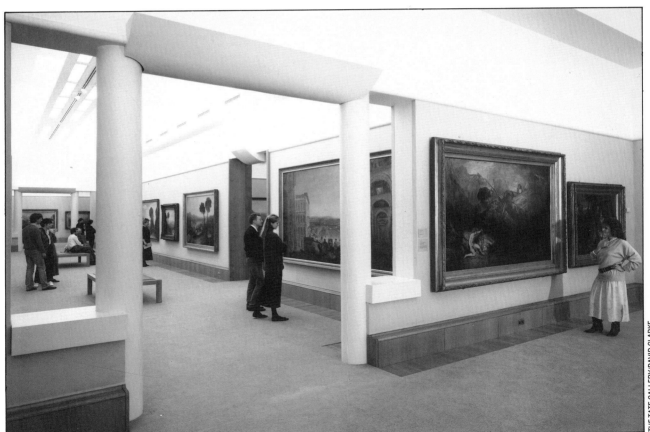

THE TATE GALLERY/DAVID CLARKE

object to the display around it. The former is therefore informative; the latter descriptive. On occasions, both labels and captions are used by exhibitors to sneak more story into the exhibition and this should be resisted. The most important thing to be remembered by the writers of labels and captions is that they must inevitably be studied at the same viewing distance as the object to which they refer. To have to look at one from five metres and the other from fifty centimetres is clearly absurd, but try telling that to the average curator in a public art gallery, where the visitors are conditioned by habit into walking three times the distance actually needed. This readability will of course govern the number of words, so we are back to the writing again. Labels must be short and precise, and written in the same way. A picture label might perhaps contain the title, the artist, the medium, the date, the size and the catalogue or collection number. If the next label starts with the size and ends with the title, there will be no order for visitors to follow subconsciously. Irritated and confused, they will probably go home.

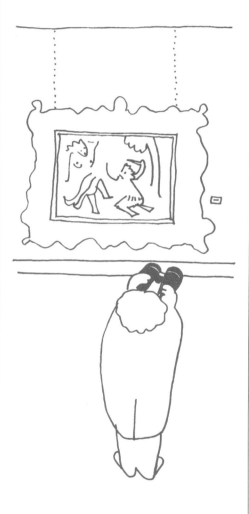

THE COPY

To many students and potential exhibition designers reading this book, the thought of actually having to write or edit anything will be anathema. It is essential to say that no designer should have to write any copy for exhibitions; a professional copywriter should be employed wherever possible. The ideal production team for a narrative or informative exhibition of any sort should contain, along with the three-dimensional designer, a graphic designer, a copywriter and a manager. In fact, despite the list of qualities considered essential for an exhibition designer, it should be remembered that these are only qualities and cannot replace professional qualifications. Any exhibition designer who does not work with, or employ, a graphic designer is always going to be operating below par and any graphic designer who takes on three-dimensional exhibition work without either training in it or extensive team experience of it will be similarly disadvantaged. Graphic design is an important and complex discipline, but even within its complexity designers are usually not specifically educated in graphic design for exhibitions. While the writer is not a graphic designer, and this book is not about graphic design, there are certain basic principles which will emerge from a discussion of the actual design of words in an exhibition.

Presentation

The most important fact to remember is that an exhibition is not a formalised method of informing. There is no such thing as a normal exhibition format, as there is with a book. A book has a clearly defined front and back, beginning and end. Its pages open on a certain side, the introduction will be at the beginning and the index at the end. Page one will always be on the right-hand side of the open spread, each page will be numbered consecutively and the print — in the western world — will read from left to

Condensed

light

medium

bold

italic

reversed out

right. Most people learn this structure from the age of three onwards, and it would never occur to them to question it. An exhibition has none of these conventions, so visitors must be given a visually strong, subconsciously recognisable, framework to enable them to find a pattern. Then they can follow the information effectively through the display area.

Information and words go hand in hand. It is almost, though not quite, impossible to communicate without them. There is a danger at this stage for those involved with commerical exhibitions to lose interest in this chapter. Please do not. No exhibition can get by without words and, instead of treating them casually, it is worth reflecting that even one or two words are better well than badly presented.

―――――――― The Print ――――――――

The letters that make the words have to be manufactured and generally printed. We read words by noticing several different elements. We read the letters, we read the shape of the whole word, we read the size of the word and we read it in direct relationship to its fellows. A letter is read by its shape. The outlines of e, a, o and q can be confused; so can r and n. Words made entirely of capitals: UPPER CASE have a less easily recognised shape than those made of upper and lower case. The former, with no tall letters (risers) or tails below the line (descenders) are not so easily read as the latter. On this page, over which you have total control, the difference is not vital, but in an exhibition where the visitor might be tired, jostled by the crowd and at the wrong distance, it becomes very important. If a fascia or title board on an exhibition is limited in size, it would therefore be well to use upper and lower case rather than the apparently more obvious capitals, in order that they should be legible from a greater distance.

Typefaces, too, make a great difference to perception. A serif is a short extra line on the arms of a letter. This E has six little extra lines, as opposed to this sans serif E. On closely packed pages, such as this one, the serif brings order, character and fluidity to the text and helps the eye along. Tests have shown that sans serif is slightly harder to read on a book page. The opposite is true if the eye is a long distance from the words, when serifs can blur the profile of a word and make it more difficult to distinguish.

Weight and spacing The weight of the print is another factor of importance. Most typefaces come in several standard packages: condensed, light, medium, bold and italic, but not all typefaces come in all packages. Correct contrast between the background and the weight of the print is important — too much contrast, like driving into bright sunlight, is eventually disturbing; too little is like driving at dusk. With white out of black, or reverse lettering — not the easiest of reading circumstances — a light typeface will disappear. If it is back-lit, bold lettering may glare. It is always best to use a heavier type than seems to be needed under reverse circumstances; so for light use medium, and never use condensed type. The photographic process employed to produce reverse print uses two negatives, so the loss of definition is twice the normal.

The spacing between the letters is crucial. It is a part of the reading process to recognise spaces: 'at' presents a familiar shape; 'a t' is unfamiliar, and confusion will reign between where one word ends and another begins. Spacing between the lines is important. It is called 'leading', after the amount of lead the old-fashioned printer would put between one line and the next. Leading should be slightly deeper in an exhibition than on the printed page and line lengths should be shorter: 50 characters maximum. The reason for both these factors is again to do with standing in an exhibition; it is impossible to stand completely still without support. The eye traverses a line, comes to the end and then flicks back and down to the next line. If the lines are too long and too densely packed, the eye quite simply gets lost on the way back and cannot find the correct place. At this point, the exhibition audience is lost. This is not psychology but fact, well remarked and recorded, for instance, in the work by Herbert Spencer and Linda Reynolds (see Bibliography), and information of great value. In the restless environment of an exhibition even

UPPER CASE

lower case

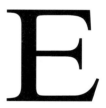

Serif

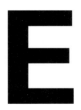

Sans serif

Close letter spacing, normal leading

Exhibitions come in all shapes and sizes. Resultantly, they mean many different things to different people.

Very close letter spacing, normal leading

Exhibitions come in all shapes and sizes. Resultantly, they mean many different things to different people.

Normal letter spacing, normal leading

Exhibitions come in all shapes and sizes. Resultantly, they mean many different things to different people.

Normal letter spacing, increased leading

Exhibitions come in all shapes and sizes. Resultantly, they mean many different things to different people.

a few words, a title, a description of a piece of machinery or a label on a photograph must be as easily received as possible.

Blocks of Text

Returning to text, we have dealt with letters, words, lines and spaces. The next item is blocks of text or paragraphs. Long paragraphs are daunting because of the apparent mass of information, and they also make it easier for the traversing eye to get lost. Start with very short paragraphs, clearly separated. Build up, but not too much, to longer paragraphs. Shape is obviously important, too; blocks of text are either justified (lined up to the left and right, as on this page) or ranged left or right (lined up to one side only). Finally, they can be centred (lined up equally on either side of an invisible centre line). Short line lengths of justified type look awful in the larger sizes used in exhibitions; they don't look too good in newspapers, either! The uneven spacing between words stands out a mile. Ranged left looks good, with the ragged right-hand edge balanced by the neat left-hand edge. If paragraphs are indented (the first line cut in by a few characters), then both sides can look messy. It is better to allow a double space between paragraphs instead. Centring can be useful, particularly when fitting text into circles or ellipses. Ranging right always looks odd, but it can be used to balance an unwieldy panel.

Ranged left...

Exhibitions come in all shapes and sizes. Resultantly, they mean many different things to different people. It is not even possible to be too specific about what the word 'exhibition' means, as it is one of those words which have several public meanings and even more 'professional' ones.

Ranged right...

Exhibitions come in all shapes and sizes. Resultantly, they mean many different things to different people. It is not even possible to be too specific about what the word 'exhibition' means, as it is one of those words which have several public meanings and even more 'professional' ones.

Centred

Exhibitions come in all shapes and sizes. Resultantly, they mean many different things to different people. It is not even possible to be too specific about what the word 'exhibition' means, as it is one of those words which have several public meanings and even more 'professional' ones.

Indented paragraph

Surprisingly enough, at the time of writing, this is the one area of exhibition design still dominated by amateurs.

Exhibitions, shows, displays, fairs are all words used to mean the same sort of thing

Line space between paragraphs

Surprisingly enough, at the time of writing, this is the one area of exhibition design still dominated by amateurs.

Exhibitions, shows, displays, fairs are all words used to mean the same sort of thing

There are no strict rules to govern the number of words in a block of main text; it rather depends upon where the text is. This leads us back to the hierarchies mentioned earlier. At a primary level there should be no paragraphs at all: just titles and headings or headlines. A secondary level might present one small and one larger paragraph, say 100 words in all. At the tertiary level, depending upon how evident the text is, quite a few paragraphs might be used. If the tertiary level is only accessed through a computer and there are plenty of them, there is really no limit.

—————————————— Scale and Distance ——————————————

The size of the display itself is obviously another controlling factor when it comes to the number of words. We have all heard stories about the Lord's Prayer being printed on the head of a pin. They are doubtless true, but then no normally sighted person would be able to read it. It is clearly possible to print as much as one likes on to an exhibit label, but if the label is 400 mm square and beside an object 450 mm behind a piece of glass and the print is 2 mm high, most people will be unable to read it. This page is controlled by you, the reader. The viewer in the exhibition is controlled by the designer. The print must be big enough to be read by the normally sighted, the myopic, far-sighted, or middle-aged and elderly. Thus the scale–distance factor is vital and can only be truly assessed by experiment, for

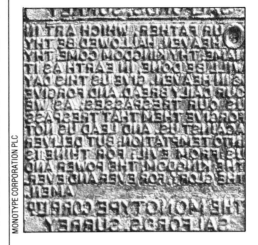

MONOTYPE CORPORATION PLC

▲ This is the Lord's Prayer on a printing block, approximately four millimetres square.

◀ Both object and label clearly legible at the same distance. 'British Fossils', Geological Museum, 1980.

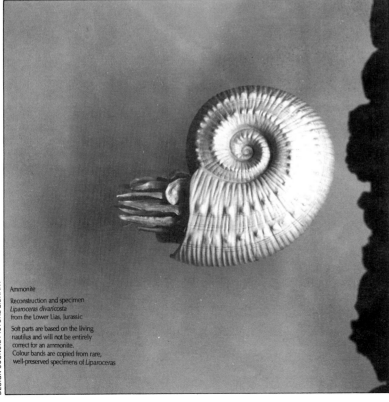

DESIGN COUNCIL PICTURE LIBRARY

Ammonite

Reconstruction and specimen
Liparoceras divaricosta
from the Lower Lias, Jurassic

Soft parts are based on the living
nautilus and will not be entirely
correct for an ammonite.
Colour bands are copied from rare,
well-preserved specimens of *Liparoceras*

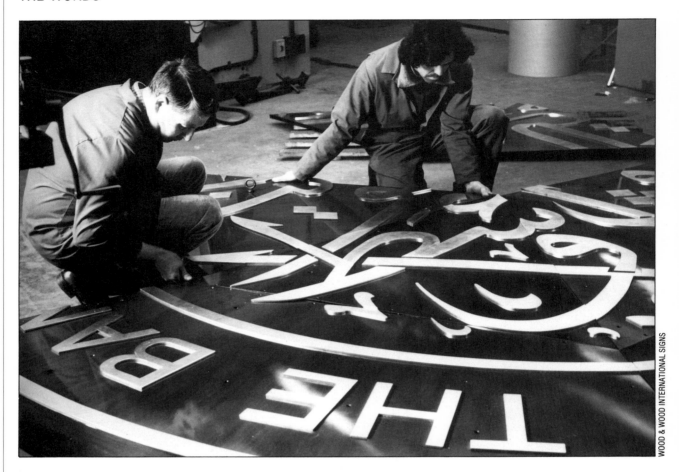

WOOD & WOOD INTERNATIONAL SIGNS

```
USES ... press a number

1... Ancient and modern uses
2... Money, Jewellery and Decoration
3... Gold and silver in electronics
4... Photography, Aerospace
5... Platinum metals in industry
6... Silver and gold reflectors
7... Precious metals in medicine

Other subjects: press G for GEOLOGY
                press E for EXTRACTION

For the SUMMARY press S
```

DESIGN COUNCIL PICTURE LIBRARY

unreadability of print varies from typeface to typeface. The size will also be affected by the ideal viewing distance of the object; pick up a pen, a ring, a cup or any nearby object and examine it. Now measure its distance from your eye — probably between 300 and 400 mm. This distance varies enormously from object to object. If there is a label describing something, it should patently be placed next to it with a reading distance that corresponds to the viewing distance. Some parts of a large object need to be examined closely, so there is a good reason for a large, remote label or title with a small relevant label beside a detailed part.

Rhythm and Consistency

All these factors need to be considered. In fact the whole exhibition should be designed with an informative rhythm which will lead to a regular and easily understood environment. To this end, a set of standardised typefaces and sizes will be selected for one exhibition in the same way as it is for a book. Main titles, headings, headlines, sub-heads and text at levels two and three will all conform to specific sizes selected to accommodate viewing distances. The main title may conform to other main titles, or be contrived to attract attention by being strikingly different.

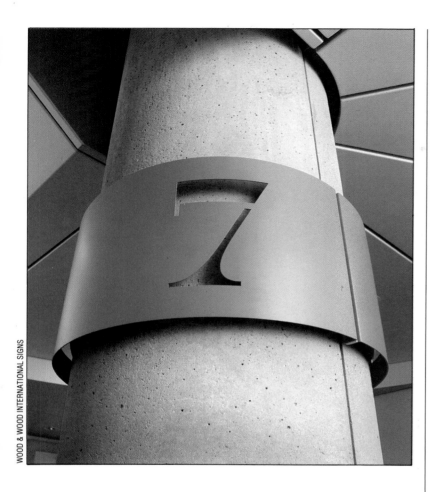

WOOD & WOOD INTERNATIONAL SIGNS

◄ Fret-cut lettering where the body of the letter is removed. Designed by Alan Fletcher for the Lloyd's Building.

◄◄ Craftsmen working on cut-brass letters.

◄ Computer-generated text (top) matched by back-lit text mimicking it below. 'Treasures of the Earth', Geological Museum, 1985.

The presentation of words is not, therefore, simple. It is complicated to make the enjoyment of an exhibition simple for the visitor. Failure to interest visitors will send them to other museums, galleries and exhibitions or to McDonald's.

Type Production

How are the words produced for an exhibition? Most of the time they are printed by conventional methods, and then copied into sizes and materials suitable for exhibitions. Printing methods change and generally improve continually, so discussion of this item is virtually pointless. However, the methods of reproducing words have remained constant for some time and will probably continue to do so, allowing for the fact that an increasing quantity of the printed word will be replaced by words generated by the computer and shown on television monitors.

The most primitive method of reproducing words at a large scale for titles or sub-titles is using cut out letters. These are cut from sheets of cork, ply, metal or plastic and painted before or after mounting them on fascias, walls or panels. It is an effective, if crude, method. The cutting precludes really good typography, but offers freedom of siting and layout. Fret-cutting letter shapes

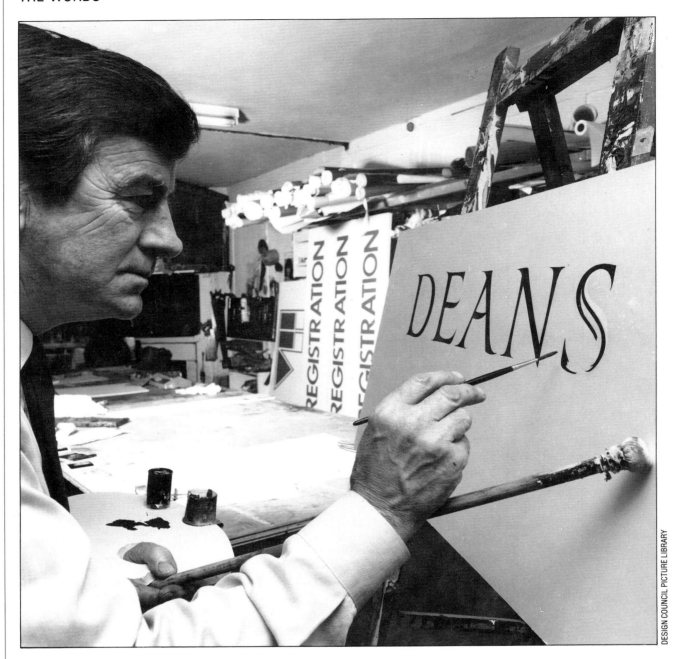

DESIGN COUNCIL PICTURE LIBRARY

▲ **Signwriting. An ancient and skilled craft still used today.**

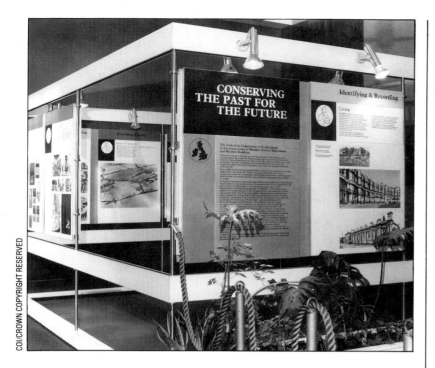

◀ A heavy-handed and dull government information display, not really helped by limp vegetation.

from a panel, leaving a hole the shape of the letter, is another good idea, but a clear plastic or glass sheet has to be glued to the back of fret-cut letters, otherwise the centres of o's and a's will fall out! These panels are generally back lit. Cut-out and fret-cut letterings do not really involve printing. The remaining techniques do, even signwriting or printing by hand-painting letters on to a surface — always executed by a skilled signwriter. The latter is an expensive, time-consuming business, but sometimes called for.

Screen printing is a method developed for mass-producing posters and fabrics. Exhibitions are peculiar because they are 'one off', so any type of printing is hardly cost effective. It must be taken for granted that important information should be put across effectively, and while hand-writing is cheap it is a most unsatisfactory method of communicating to a large audience. Screen printing is a technique whereby a stencil is made from fine cloth, parts of which are sealed with size or glue. Ink is squeezed through the stencil and on to the object to be printed. It is at its best when used for printing colour on to colour. To use it for black and white is generally a waste of money.

Photostats (enlarged photographs of specially printed text) are more than adequate when heat-sealed for all temporary and most permanent exhibitions. In large areas of brightly lit informative displays colour, for instance, brown printed on to biege, is far less aggressive, and therefore less difficult to read, than black on white. Also colour can be used for both applying graphic rhythm and punctuation. For example, headings could be printed in one colour, text in another, and words which might merit quotation marks printed instead in another colour. Captions to over-mounted pictures or diagrams might be printed in a different colour, thus separating body text from labels. There are very satisfactory ways of printing photographic enlargements in colour, but only on to white, or on to a coloured ground providing there is a white separation between the colours. Using both these methods imaginatively can lead to a well-ordered and attractive display, encouraging the visitor to take an interest in the information presented, *and* making it easy to follow.

Order and Decoration

Order, of course, is important, but too much is sterile and forbidding. Again balance is the thing and, if deemed necessary,

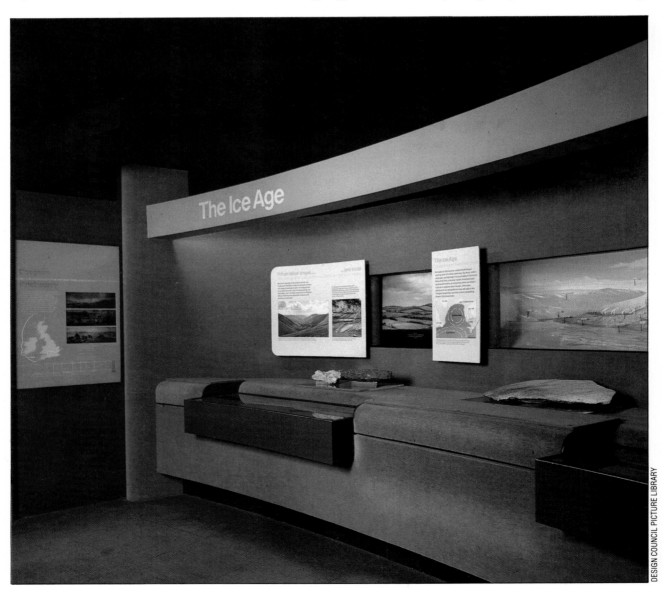

▼ 'Britain before Man'. Geological Museum, 1977. Colour is used to unify the graphics and help in the rhythmic flow of information.

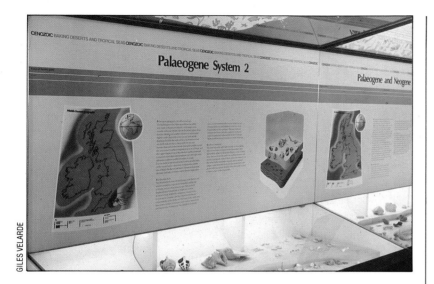

GILES VELARDE

◀ Decoration used to separate tiers in a hierarchy of information. 'British Fossils', Geological Museum, 1980.

◀ Colour and illustration used to brighten an otherwise dull display. A portable exhibition designed for the British Geological Survey, 1985.

GILES VELARDE

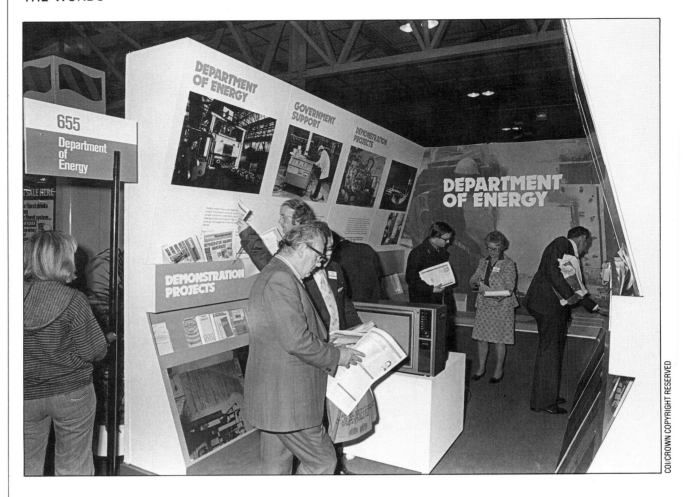

▲ Untidy, overbearing graphics to which, not surprisingly, nobody is paying any attention.

decoration. When a mass of information is presented, too much order can make it sinister and dull. When it is chaotic, it looks like hard work.

A median path must be sought by the graphic designer in conjunction with the three-dimensional designer. There is a band of normal vision from 900 mm to 2000 mm from the floor which should normally contain all detailed information; decoration can emphasise that band and ensure that the eye stays within it or, when required, rise above or sink below it. But, decoration has to be *used*; it must never be there on a whim, for one person's decoration is another's ghastly mess. It is an insupportable argument if taste is the only criterion. Taste, as a word, is meaningless because it conveys something different from every speaker to every listener. It is a word abused by overuse. When decoration is employed it is there for a purpose: to enliven thematically a poorly illustrated story; to delineate chapters of the story; to enable the important graphics to over-ride a dull shell scheme or system; to create a special, individual atmosphere. Decoration should be restrained, and used always slightly less than required. If the decoration dominates the information, the message will be

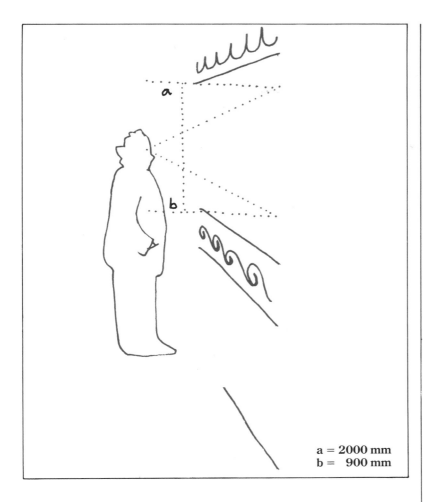

a = 2000 mm
b = 900 mm

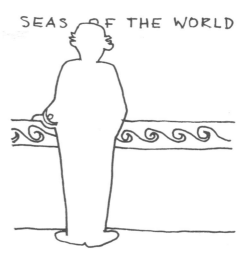

▲ **Decoration used to emphasise the boundaries of important information.**

◄ **The normal band of vision within which important information should be placed.**

lost. Exhibitions are not for designers to show everybody how clever they are.

─────────── Detailed Presentation ───────────

All text, and the objects and pictures associated with it, should be presented at easy right angles to the eye. This means that if the visitor has to look down or up to 'read', the displays should remain at right angles to the eye (see illustration). Once angles are involved — any angles — the relationship of light sources to these flat planes becomes important, in order that reflections or glare can be avoided (see illustration). Pictures are associated with text in a number of ways. They can be mounted on independent blocks and then displaced on a wall. They can be mounted on panels with the text on a strip below. They can have the text overmounted. They can be produced on a separate negative and the two merged in printing. Finally, they can all be assembled on the same panel, the words on one master photostat with the pictures mounted separately. In this last method, remember that no two whites are ever the same; therefore diagrams out of a white ground will look like a bad patch when stuck on to a white

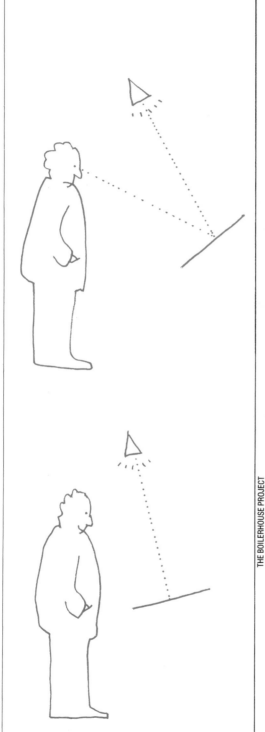

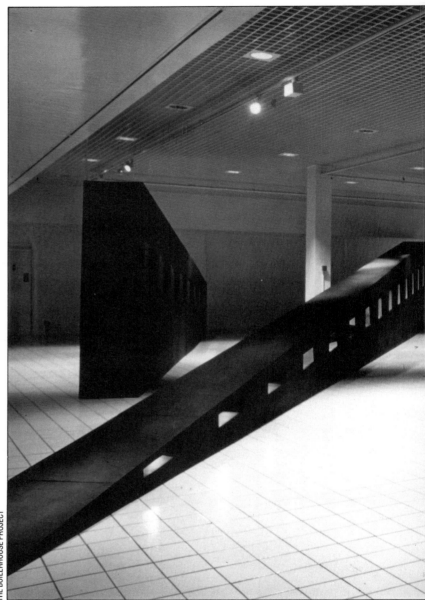

THE BOILERHOUSE PROJECT

photostat. It is best if the diagram is reversed out of black, grey or a colour. Captions and labels should be differentiated, the former describing the object using text and the latter giving the essential basic information: size, weight, provenance, code number, artist or manufacturer in staccato, listed form. All captions should be of a similar character and length, and always appear in the same relationship to the object throughout any given exhibition. All labels should present their information in the same order and style, and also relate similarly to the objects.

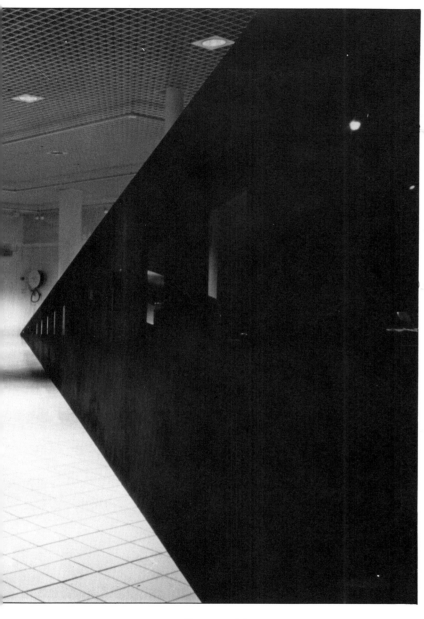

◀ **Clearly absurd exhibition design wherein only a few of the showcases come anywhere near acceptable viewing heights. Hand Tools exhibition at the Boilerhouse, London, 1984.**

Composition

All pictures have a compositional direction. A well-composed diagram or picture will draw the eye to the centre, the point of sharpest vision and therefore detail. Many photographs, however, have an implied direction. The most obvious is when it is of something that moves — an animal, car or ship for instance. The eye will be led in the direction of normal movement. Some compositions have a strong, dark form to one side with perspective lines leading arrow-like to a pale sky on the other; this 'arrow' is subliminally perceived. These markers should be used to lead the visitor's eye smoothly in the direction of the informa-

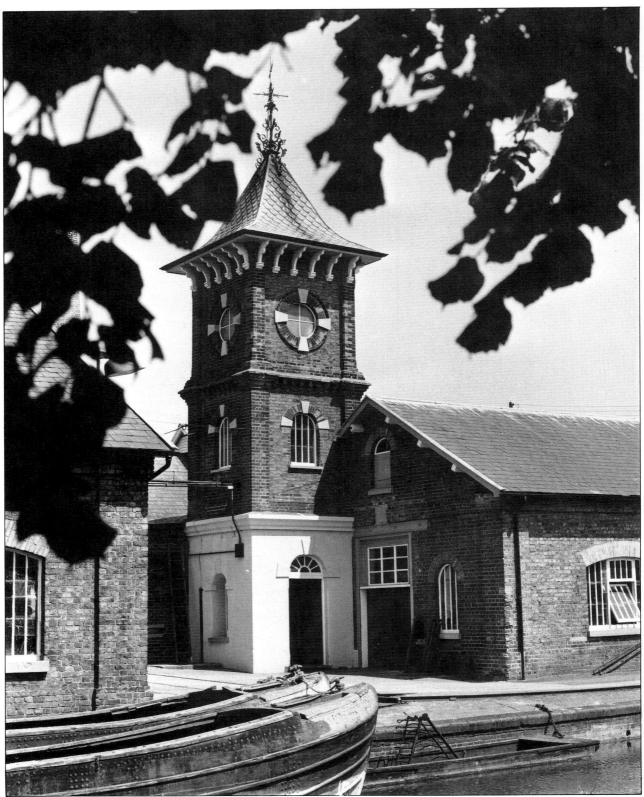

DEREK PRATT

tion run — left to right in the West, for we read from left to right.

Clearly there is scope for a whole book about exhibition graphics, going into considerable detail about design, typography, reproduction methods and techniques. This chapter attempts only to be a guide to an exhibition designer — a three-dimensional designer — to give an understanding of the need for professional graphic design input and, more importantly, knowledge of how to brief, control and supervise the graphics to create a harmonious whole. Whereas it is usually the three-

◀ A well-composed, if uninspiring, picture where the eye is lead peacefully towards the centre.

▼ A picture that would look uneasy on the left of a display panel but fine on the right.

SUSAN TRANGMAR

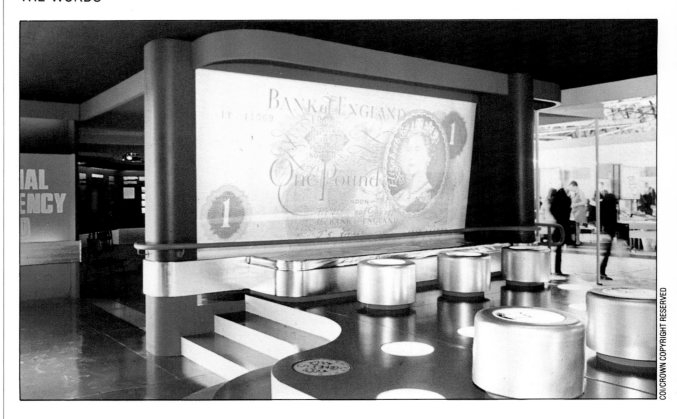

▲ A stand designed deliberately to reflect the fashion of the late sixties and thus give decimalisation a thoroughly modern image.

dimensional designer who accepts a brief for an exhibition, it is valuable if a graphic designer is consulted at the earliest possible moment; in fact as soon as a three-dimensional form to the exhibition emerges. In this way, the graphic input will be sympathetic and relevant.

Fashion

This is a good point at which to consider one aspect of design that strongly affects both three-dimensional and graphic design: fashion. Fashion plays an important role in the commercial and aesthetic part of our lives. However, it is transient. Its transience and immediate relevance must therefore be clearly considered, and either dismissed or used. If an exhibition is to be permanent, then it is far more important that it should 'look' aesthetically relevant for as long as possible. The same applies to the graphics in the exhibition, for there are distinct fashions in typeface and style of embellishment. If a 'timeless' design is attempted for an exhibition, then the graphics will let it down if full of fashionable typefaces and quirks. Typefaces should be selected for their stylistic relevance to the subject and decoration should be designed similarly. It is of course almost impossible to exclude fashion from any design but it should, in these permanent circumstances, be only a gentle reminder of the period of execution and not a dominant statement.

When a temporary structure is envisaged, fashion can be used and even graphics and decoration set in the style. When a very recent development is being exhibited, then it is positively beneficial for the exhibition to be as stylish as possible, thus reflecting the modernity of the product and the company image. These are two clear examples; the sensitive and imaginative designer will be aware of fashion and use it — or, with luck, create it — to serve the purpose of the exhibition.

––––––––––––––––––––

Words are fundamental ingredients of exhibition design. This chapter has attempted to explain that both the content and the presentation of words should be considered by the designer from the earliest point of involvement. It is useless to discuss them as an unfortunate necessity, to be added as crude labels or stuck on displays at the last moment. They should be integrated and homogeneous. The plan, the very layout of the exhibition, should harmonise with the informative content to this end.

(a)

(b)

(c)

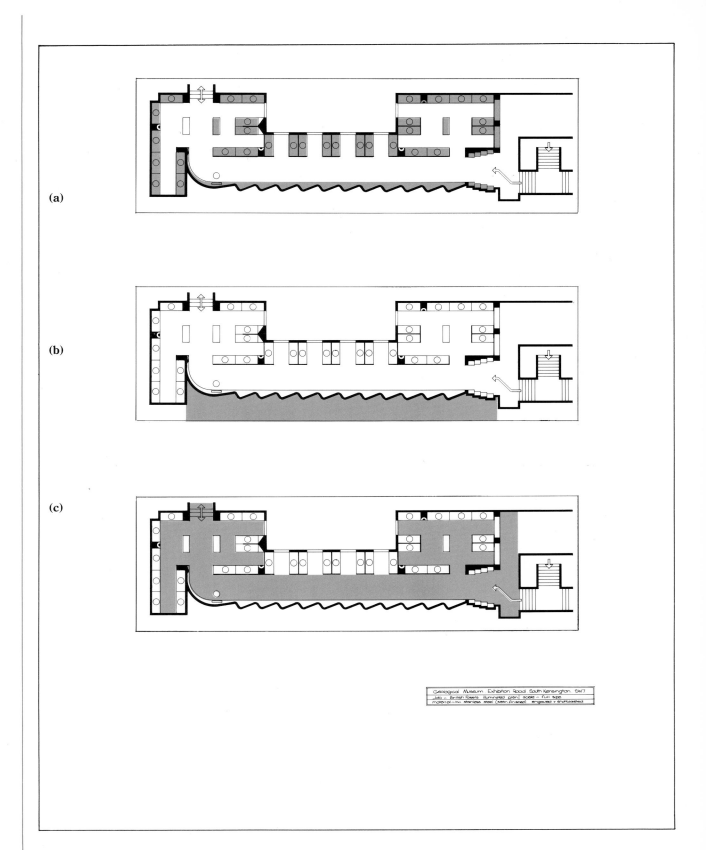

Geological Museum Exhibition Road South Kensington SW7
Job – British Fossils illuminated plan scale – full size
material–1mm stainless steel (satin finished) engraved + shotblasted

5
THE DESIGN

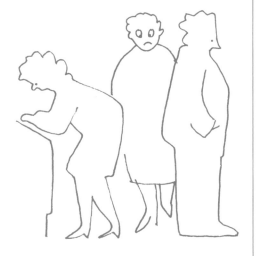

Designing is problem solving. No problem can be effectively dealt with until it has been defined. Chapter 3, entitled 'The Brief', attempted to set out the essential elements of the problem and the design process logically follows from that. There is, and always will be, one imponderable element among those under consideration: the visitor, the person for whom the exhibition is ultimately designed. Research is going on to attempt to describe the potential behaviour of this elusive creature and this will be discussed in a later chapter, but it is vital for the designer to remember that the most valuable tool available when it comes to visitor assessment is personal observation. Observation, used constructively, is essential to good design. It is one thing to skim through glossy magazines on a search for ideas or stimulation, but it is quite another to visit exhibitions and notice both the design and the visitors' reaction to it. Habitual observation of this kind will build up a valuable body of experience, often described as intuition but actually priceless knowledge — which cannot be categorised as scientific knowledge. The danger with scientifically acquired information based on visitor questioning is that it is inevitably subjective (two people cannot communicate without a whole sub-stratum of influences) and it is assumed to be fact. The danger with observed information is that it is assumed to be guesswork. There is an area of visitor research waiting to be undertaken where careful observations by designers are scientifically recorded and prepared. Meanwhile, however, the total use of three-dimensional space must be planned effectively.

PLANNING

For the sake of this chapter, planning means drawing a scale plan and fitting on to it the necessary parts and spaces to form an exhibition.

Public Space

This is the area of the exhibition devoted to the movement and use of the public. It must be easily and immediately accessible and it must be big enough for them. Most doorways, for example, are big enough for people to pass through alone but not really for people to pass each other. There are books about 'human dimensions', but sheer commonsense and a measuring tape will dictate the width of an aisle in which one person may be standing, looking or bending to look, while two others are passing behind.

◀ **Plan for 'British Fossils',
Geological Museum, 1980, showing
(a) exhibition space,
(b) administrative space and
(c) public space.**

83

There must be room for people to talk and to exchange information without disturbing the solitary viewer.

Informative Space

This is the actual exhibition space for objects, models, artefacts, showcases, light-boxes and vertical or sloping flat displays. Obviously, the available space is somewhat controlled by the size of the objects on display. Moreover it must be planned with its informative and attractive values in mind; if all the most inviting objects are placed on the edge of an exhibition, the visitor is going to be very disappointed when moving into the duller spaces beyond. Size is important, of course; huge objects can obscure small ones. Safety is important; if working exhibits are involved there must be a barrier and a space between them and the visitor.

Administrative Space

This is space set aside for many vital purposes out of direct reach or sight of the public. It is space for access for maintenance changing bulbs behind transparencies or lamps for projectors, o' attending to working exhibits or models. Many exhibitions have counters where administrative space meets public space; these must be adroitly sited and ought to be provided with solid fronts, so that tired attendants can relax their legs and feet out of sight of the visitor.

Space for storage Many temporary exhibitions are backed up with literature and samples to be given away, so an assessment of these needs is important.

Space for staff Most temporary exhibitions have attendant managers and representatives who need space to relax, loosen collars, have a cup of tea or change into uniforms. No matter how small the stand, such space is vital. On huge temporary stands — at world fairs, for example — this space can run into a sizeable proportion of the whole area, calling for washrooms, offices, changing rooms and kitchens.

Entertainment space Additional space might be required for important customers to be given special treatment, such as drinks or private video shows.

Types of Plan

Essentially, there are two broad types of arrangement: extrovert and introvert.

The extrovert exhibition This type is built on an island or near-island all to itself, either in an exhibition hall, a museum or an outdoor site. At their grandest, these extrovert exhibitions could be pavilions at world fairs. This is a form of design which appeals for attention from all sides and is frequently open to the public on all sides. Its displays are designed to attract the public 'on board', as it were. In exhibition halls these stands can be double-deckers, two- or even three-floored structures presenting vast and exotic façades to compete with their neighbours in attracting public attention. If they present huge blank walls to the public, they are denying the value of the island site (which costs more to rent); therefore the space should be either at the heart or upper level of such a stand, or on an unimportant elevation. Every aspect of the design should encourage the public to visit. This type of design can be difficult to supervise, not only from the point of view of security, but also from the commercial standpoint. It is essential that every visitor be visible to the stand staff, who can then approach at the right moment if a sale looks possible. Stands of this nature are frequently costly affairs, so the financial burden of extra staff with their attendant travel and subsistence requirements ought to be considered at the outset.

The introvert exhibition This type presents less of a problem for supervision. It refers to an exhibition designed into an existing space — a booth at a trade fair; a room or suite of rooms in a museum, gallery or hotel. Here, there are only internal spaces

▼ The National Gallery in London. A gallery plan that inevitably encourages introverted exhibitions.

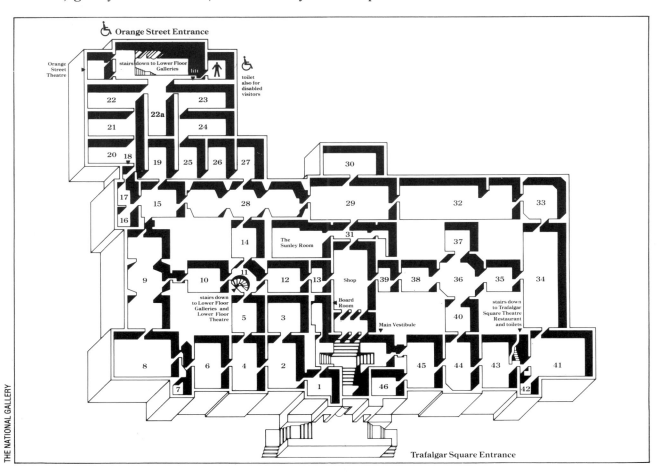

and surfaces to be thought about, with possibly only one outside elevation. As the visitors come and go, they pass either through the front of the booth or the entrance and exit to the rooms. In an introvert exhibition, the challenge is to get the visitors through the entrance and, once there, to keep them interested since it is not so easy to leave the area. This is particularly true in a suite of adjoining rooms in a gallery. Some galleries, the Royal Academy in London, for instance, were deliberately designed with interconnecting spaces, often on four sides. This facilitates the design of temporary exhibitions, all introverted, of many sizes and rooms are sealed off or included as and when required.

Planning Considerations

Supervision The importance of supervision has already been mentioned. In the late 1960s it meant simply that it had to be possible to see all parts of an exhibition from one or two vantage points so that, in the commercial venue, visitors could be persuaded to buy by the salesmen. In the last decade, supervision has come to mean guarding against vandals and, at worst, terrorists. A well-designed exhibition is one whose sales and/or security staff can see through, round or over the exhibits and the informative space.

Control One other effect arises from this consideration. Convoluted plans are tiresome for the visitor. He or she is not there to try and find the way around, but to be easily confronted by the things the exhibitor wants to be seen and appreciated. If it is made difficult the visitor will not bother — therefore there are good and bad plans. Good and bad are of course emotive and subjective words, but such plans exist and have nothing to do with taste. A good plan is either subconsciously or consciously easy to follow; visitors know where they are, relative to the exhibition and the world outside, feel consequently more at ease, and so more receptive to the information displayed. It should always be possible for visitors to identify familiar landmarks. They then remain oriented and in control. Exhibits should be placed in a logical sequence. All subjects have information patterns or structures to their description, and once the designer has arrived at one such pattern it should be adhered to. A petrol engine, for instance, can be described historically by its evolution from invention to the present day; or sociologically through the immense variety of its uses and its effect on society; or chemically by referring to the component minerals that go to make it up. Clearly, one or more of these information patterns will be relevant to its presence on display and pertinent to the story being told. Accordingly the objects on display relevant to the engine must be laid out in the relevant order. Confusion eventually leads to despair, and a despairing visitor makes a very poor customer.

This confusion is rampant in a bad plan. Such a plan will be disconcerting and maze-like. It could be dauntingly large with no clear sign of display activity, so that it is difficult for the visitor to know whether or not entry is allowed, whether to touch or not. A bad plan shows no clear difference between public, exhibit and administrative space and it is full of apparent blind alleys or culs-de-sac. The administrative space can be so forbidding and vast that it presents a grim exterior to the public, even if sounds of hilarity can be heard from behind the wall. A bad plan ought to be evident on the drawing board. A good plan will elevate well from the drawing to the site, to present a friendly and receptive structure in which the assimilation of information comes naturally and easily to the visitor.

Vertical Treatment

Limitless height is not a commodity generally available to the exhibition designer and, even if it were, it would not be of any great value except as a place in which to indicate one's presence. The vital thing to remember with vertical space is that the more there is of it, the further away the visitor has to be in order to see it. The Eiffel Tower, that ultimate exhibition feature, can be seen in grossly distorted detail from close to, and only in the most general possible way from about a mile away. There is no in-between. If you wanted to study its complex structure about halfway up, you would have to contrive all sorts of devices to enable you to do so. Average eye level is considered to be about

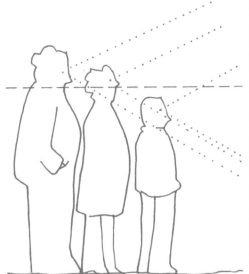

▲ Average eye level is said to be about 1600mm from the floor. It does not suit everybody, but nothing is perfect.

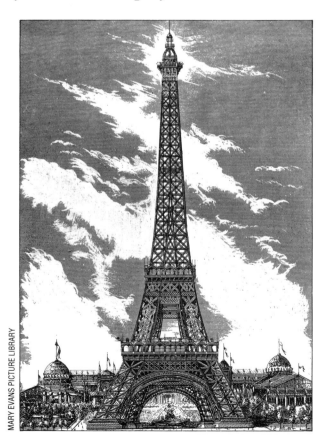

MARY EVANS PICTURE LIBRARY

◄ The first of Man's aspiring exhibition features — but you have to be a long way off to see it properly.

1600 mm above floor level. If a vertical display panel is approximately a metre high and a metre off the ground, the viewer will have to be about a metre away from it to view or 'read' a square metre of it comfortably. If the display has to start near floor level and rise to three metres up, then it must first be seen from at least three metres away. After the initial vertical appreciation, the visitor can move in closely to examine it in more detail. If there is no way that the correct viewing distance can be provided, then there is no point in putting on such a display, except in those instances where the sheer scale of an object can be emphasised by exaggeration when it is placed in close confines. Obviously in the exhibition context vertical and horizontal space is inextricably intertwined and, as was seen in the last chapter, readability of words has a considerable effect on the acceptability or otherwise of certain contrived spaces.

Horizontal Treatment

Horizontal space is not divided up necessarily by solid verticals, solid walls or solid exhibits; transparent or semi-open walls and objects are generally far friendlier things than the opaque mat-

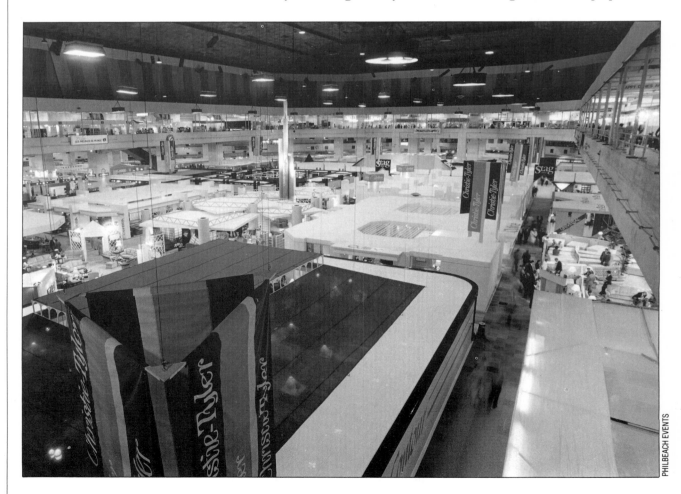

PHILBEACH EVENTS

erials that are usually found in buildings. Double-sided showcases can also form divisions, as can low horizontal cases or displays; thus a plan, a devised flow of visitors in certain informative directions, can generally be contrived as much by the placement of objects as by the displacement of artificial walls and open or solid partitions.

It is this use of vertical space that, mixed with a well-devised plan, allows for two of the most important elements in any exhibition: fluid circulation, and ease of supervision. Fluid circulation is vital for the comfortable and logical reception of information in space. Good supervision is vital to the exhibition staff to avoid missing customers and to security staff so that, if the occasion arises, they can prevent damage or theft. Of course if the potential thief or vandal never feels alone, he is unlikely to attempt anything.

The Exhibits

Without objects, there would be no need for this book. Exhibitions are essentially about objects. In the museum context they are paramount, for it is only in museums that the image-saturated

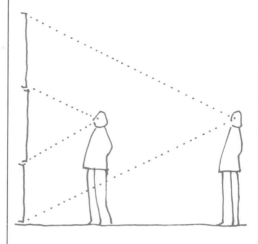

◄◄ **International Furniture Exhibition, Earls Court, 1987.**

◄ **Cleverly contrived double-sided showcases. 'Man's Place in Evolution', British Museum (Natural History), 1980.**

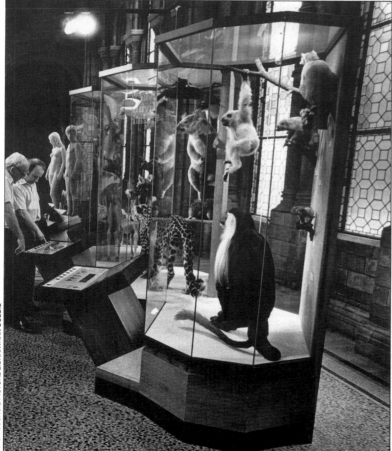

► **Scale models lending drama to a display.**

▼ **Standing the world on its side to emphasise a point.**

and more or less sedentary public can see, relate to and sometimes touch things they have read about or seen pictures of elsewhere. A museum exhibition without objects is therefore almost offensive and its *raison d'être* must be questionable. Where what is clearly only a words-and-pictures narrative can be told in a three-dimensional situation, in the absence of artefacts, models and replicas have to be made. In the commercial or prestige exhibition, objects lend integrity and interest to the statements made about them, but paradoxically it is frequently the statements which are most important. The visitor is therefore drawn to the statements through the objects. A car is a car is a car, but the facts about fuel consumption, power and performance can only be stated and not tested by the visitor. It is the gleaming, polished example that attracts attention to these important selling points. At a prestige exhibition, a national pavilion for example, products of the nation — even if only beautifully

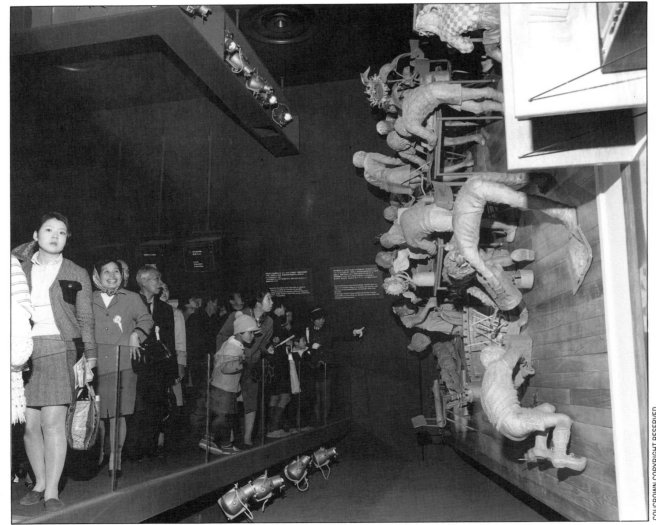

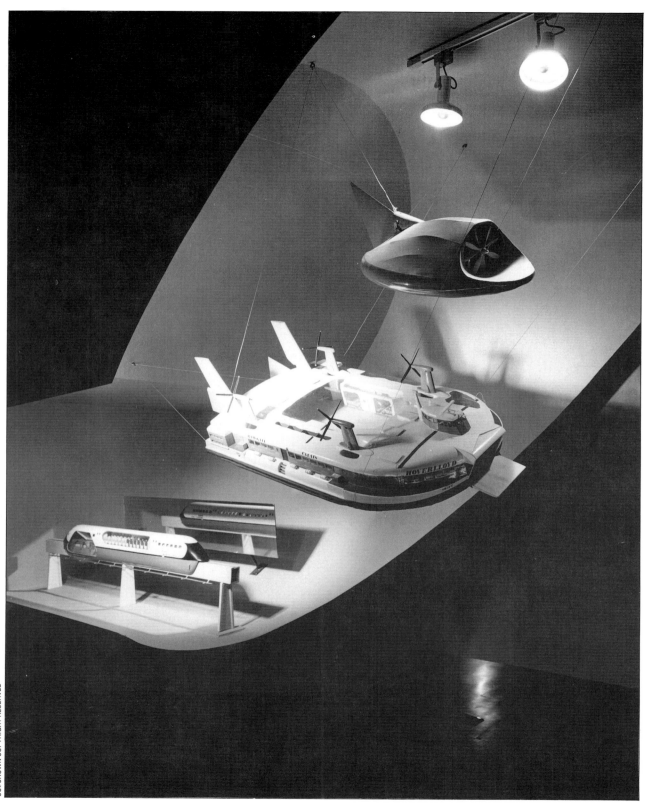

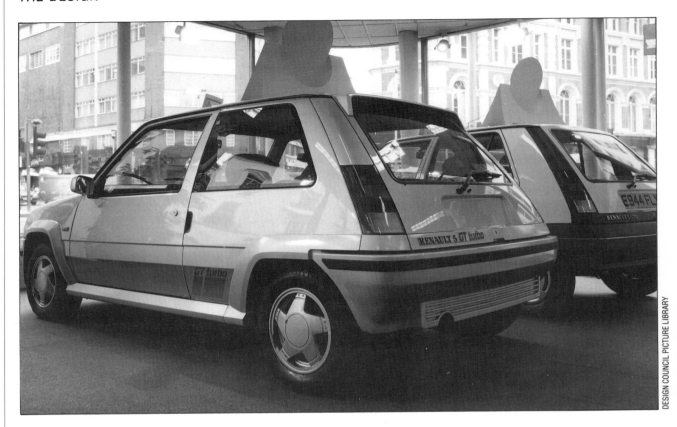

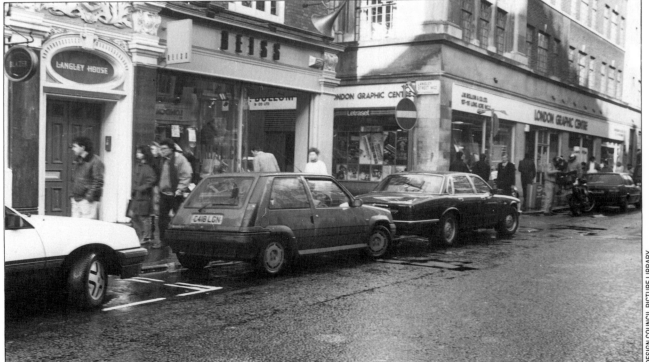

displayed — give the attendant statements an air of conviction. A pavilion totally devoid of objects of this kind occasionally can be of interest but it is rare. The average visitor does not pay the entrance fee, and travel sometimes hundreds of miles, only to be told something which could easily be read in a magazine or encyclopaedia. There is a magic to displayed objects which is hard to explain. An ordinary car, polished, tilted and lit for display has a charisma quite unlike that of the very same vehicle parked in the road.

The size or scale of exhibits is also important. The very large and the very small always create a peculiar interest. Their context is equally important. A very large object on a huge exhibition stand will simply look normal, but if it is apparently cramped in, its scale will be exaggerated. Similarly, very small objects shown individually in special cases will have their smallness and their value enhanced by this special treatment. Massing ordinary objects also gives them a special charm. Chinese national pavilions over the years have ignored contemporary display techniques

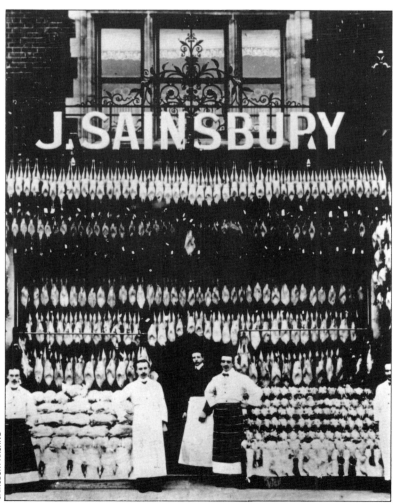

SAINSBURY ARCHIVE

◄◄ Paraded in the showroom the car will attract attention . . .

◄◄ . . . while in the street it is not given a second glance.

◄ Which is more attractive, the display or the objects on display?

and shown the variety and interest of their products by massing them on tiered displays like Victorian grocers' shops. The sheer quantity and neatness of the goods seem to add to their quality, while emphasising the productivity of the country of origin. Contrast emphasises size. Magnified models of small objects or small models of huge things always generate interest and, as all movement attracts the eye, making objects of all sizes revolve is another way of emphasising their qualities and attracting attention. We have all experienced the great delight of examining exquisitely detailed workmanship, and it is building valuable information upon these pleasurable responses that makes for good exhibition display.

Information

Information must be the basis upon which all exhibition planning eventually takes place. After all the practical considerations, it is the information that decides the general layout. The synopsis of the information provided with the brief must be clear and sufficiently finalised for the layout to be decided at a comparatively early stage.

There are two fundamental ways of displaying or retailing information (other, of course, than chaotically or informally). A systematic display will be laid out in some explicit order — chronological, scientific, biological or evolutionary. A thematic display will be laid out as a story, around a central theme. There has been a strong move towards essentially thematic displays in recent years. 'Story' titles make evocative and inviting exhibition themes. Moreover they provide something for the visitor's imagination to dwell upon. The two methods can easily be mixed so that a thematic exhibition, built around a theme or story, can be chronologically ordered. This ordering of the exhibition will obviously affect the planning of the exhibition site. Even the very smallest booth will need to have the layout of the information considered, but clearly the larger and more complex the site, the more important the logical layout becomes. On an island site, a logical plan can be difficult to achieve since the visitors will approach from all directions; so various devices have to be contrived to encourage passage in the direction the designer wants. The best way of achieving this is to place the most eye-catching display at the beginning of the story. It must be attractive — literally in the way that a lighted candle attracts a moth. Having attracted the visitor in this way, the problem is only partly solved; he or she must then be encouraged to proceed in the direction of the informative path by orienting displays in such a manner that can be followed easily. (This was dealt with in detail in the preceding chapter.) With a systematic display on an island site, the information can be placed in concentric circles around the exhibition in such a way that the starting or ending place does not really matter.

A visitor cannot easily be coerced; the public responds badly to formalised and compulsory routes. People bunch up in the least

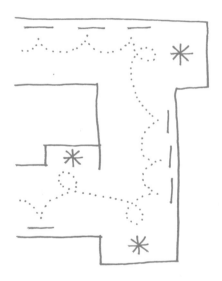

▲ The visitor will be attracted by powerful displays (∗) and pictures or text panels leading from left to right.

expected places, and the end result, in a popular exhibition, is a controlled queue: not the best way to sell products or encourage learning. At world fairs, this bunched queuing has become almost a way of life in the more popular pavilions, though the public at world fairs is often of the least discriminating kind. It is nevertheless bad design to create a situation in which people — no matter how sheepishly — plod slowly around any exhibition, being forced to see the displays at the pace of the queue and not at their own. Freedom of movement through objects and information should be fundamental to good design. It is not only bad design to end up with such a queue, but also bad co-ordination between the publicists and the organisers. Frequently an exhibition is 'hyped' way beyond its ability to cope. The organisers and sponsors delightedly see huge queues going to see their exhibition, but it is questionable whether such a solid phalanx of eventually cross and uncomfortable visitors is actually good publicity at all. To be forced to stand in front of the same picture that one does not particularly like cannot, in the long term, leave one with a kindly feeling.

Illustration

Illustrations form a fundamental part of any exhibition. To many people, exhibitions are simply about pictures, but it is the picture which is on exhibition in its own right. Pictures also play what might be termed secondary and tertiary roles. The secondary role is when pictures of the exhibits are on display. One fine object is backed up by photographs of other varieties or types of the same thing. The tertiary role is when they form part of the background to, or explanation of, the objects. Pictures in the primary role, as in an art exhibition, are generally seen to be outside the remit of the designer. In this context, the design brief may be simply to create a tasteful, well-lit background while others — art historians, for example — take care of the hanging within the shell that the designer has created. This can lead to a situation where the exhibition is totally out of control. Pictures are placed within their historical context perhaps, but their placement bears no relation to the actual planning of the exhibition. If the designer does not know the whereabouts of this or that picture, with this or that viewing distance and pulling power, it is impossible to plan an exhibition to function satisfactorily. Any exhibition is a machine for enlightenment. If the working parts are simply thrown together on the ground, how can it possibly work? Recently exhibitions of fine art in the UK have virtually all been chaotic, inhospitable environments wherein the public struggles for information, in circumstances arranged to please an élite few who only experience the exhibition in the comfort of a private view.

Pictures in their secondary or tertiary roles are in the place where we start to get involved with the nitty-gritty of informative display. Everything so far in this chapter has been in general terms, but when discussing the process of actually informing the

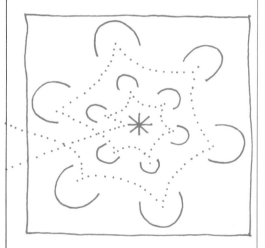

▲ The visitor will be attracted by a powerful central display (∗) and will then move outwards past other highlights not too apparent from the outside.

visitor with pictures and objects, we need to talk about the actual methods of presenting them.

The simplest and cheapest method is the photograph, black and white, mounted on cardboard at a standard size. It is clearly worth spending a bit of money, first of all, on using colour, and secondly on enlarging the photograph at least to a suitable viewing size relative to the object it adjoins. Of course, enlargements can be taken to glorious extremes, depending on paper size, but it must be remembered that the quality of the original negative becomes more and more critical the bigger the enlargement becomes. A 35 mm negative, enlarged to two metres across, becomes very grainy, which is acceptable provided that effect

▼ A photograph enlarged for background effect.

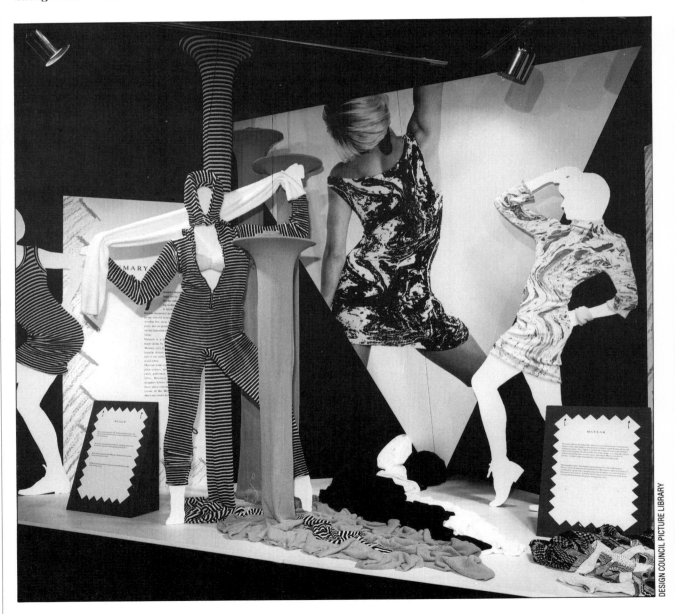

only is required and the visitor is not expected to examine it closely for detailed information. These enlargements are generally on plastic-coated paper, wet-mounted on to panels. The paper comes only in specified widths, so the joints in the enlargement over a certain size have to be considered. The length of the rolls of paper is generally unlimiting, so only one set of joints has to be watched. If they are lit along the seam, there will be no shadow, but if light falls across the seam the joint can become quite obvious. It is also possible to enlarge on to transparent plastic film, either for normal viewing or for back lighting. The size of these plastic sheets again varies, but they are usually a great deal larger and costlier than photographic paper, and require a strong supporting frame to stretch the film.

Back-lit transparencies on proper film, sandwiched between opal and clear glass or Perspex sheets and lit with a carefully mounted battery of fluorescent tubes at least 200 mm back from the film, are generally considered to be the best way of showing good quality colour photographs in an exhibition. The size is limited to the sheet film size, so it is generally within the enlargement range of the original negative. However, the bigger the size, the better. Photographs can also be enlarged by computer reading methods on to cloth, stretched or used as a curtain, and carpet. Again, there is a considerable loss of definition, so enlargements of this type can only be used for scene-setting or background purposes. Photographs on to cloth have the advantage of being completely non-reflective; there are no high spots of light to irritate the visitor. Other materials that will receive photographs are plastic laminates in which the photograph is printed on to a special tissue and then laminated either into a thermoplastic or glass-reinforced plastic. These laminates can be made almost indestructible. Photographs reproduced in many of the above methods can be moved or interchanged, so that more than one picture can occupy the same apparent space. Prints can be displayed on mechanical flip-over panels, virtually a picture book with hard pages, or transparencies can be contained on a long opal reel that, to predetermined pulses, advances picture by picture. These devices are a patented French system called 'Rotosign'. Pictures can also be mounted on what are called 'toblerones', after the triangular-sectioned chocolate bars. Either a single picture is mounted on to each face of the toblerone, which revolves mechanically, stopping and starting for each face, or many toblerones can be racked vertically or horizontally with the photograph sliced and mounted on to them. If the whole rack is revolved continuously, the changing picture effect can be quite dramatic. This method is also used in a commercial product called Rotagraphics, but the 20 mm slats with 2 mm joints degrade the photograph somewhat.

While so far only considering photographs, this section does of course include pictures, diagrams, maps etc, often turned into photographs for ease of reproduction. However, photographs are not always the solution to the problems of either detailed or

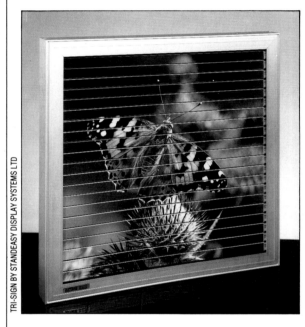

TRI-SIGN BY STANDEASY DISPLAY SYSTEMS LTD

▲ **Tri-sign moving picture.**

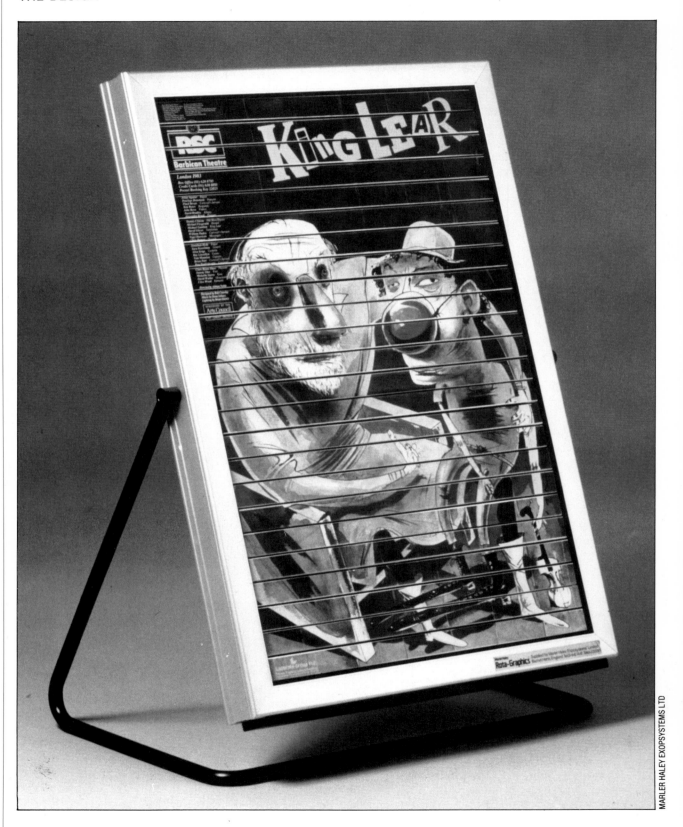

background illustration. Murals are often considered to fulfil the need for large scale, scene-setting artwork both for commercial ventures and prestige or museum exhibitions. In scientific or archaeological displays, representation of the scenery or way of life, or artefacts of centuries ago, can often best be expressed in this way. Special artwork is often commissioned from specialist illustrators and mural artists who work closely with academics and reference materials, to produce detailed and accurate repre-

◀ The triangular section horizontal bars move through 120 degrees to show three separate pictures in the same space.

▼ A photo mural at a commercial exhibition. Furneaux Stewart's stand for Porsche at the Motor Show, 1986, NEC.

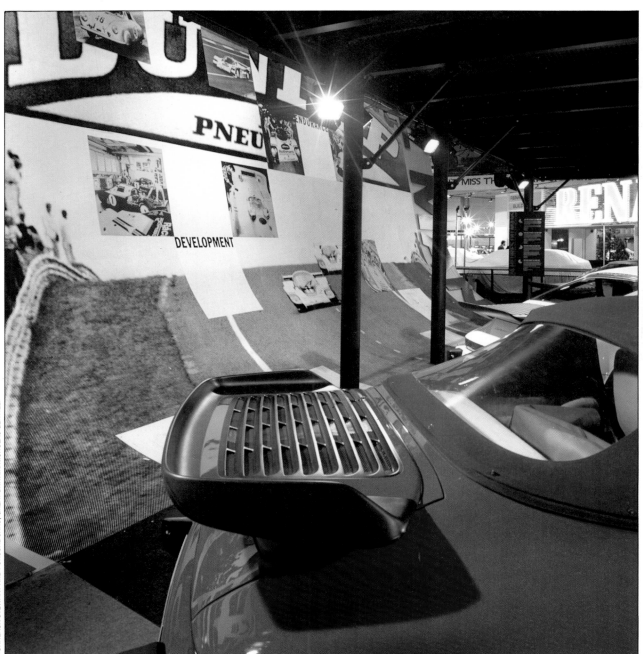

sentations. Glass painting, these days generally hand painted on to clear acrylic sheets, gives a three-dimensional effect sometimes very subtle and full of depth. They, more than other illustratons, have to be specially lit and the artists themselves often undertake to light them. Another form of flat illustration frequently used is the cut-away diagram, again the work of a specialist. This shows the inner workings of anything from a flea to a diesel engine. Maps are often a necessity, either to show distribution networks or natural locations. The normal map, produced by cartographic organisations, is generally quite useless for exhibition purposes, being designed with a totally different reading circumstance in mind; special maps have therefore to be

▶ An underwater scene painted on eight layers of acrylic sheet. A skilfully executed 'glass painting' in the 'Britain before Man' exhibition, Geological Museum, 1977.

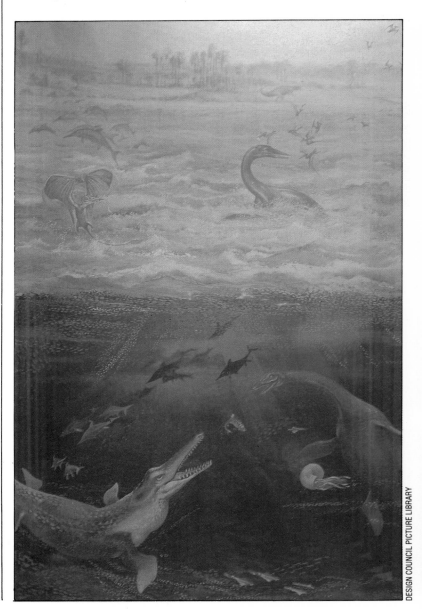

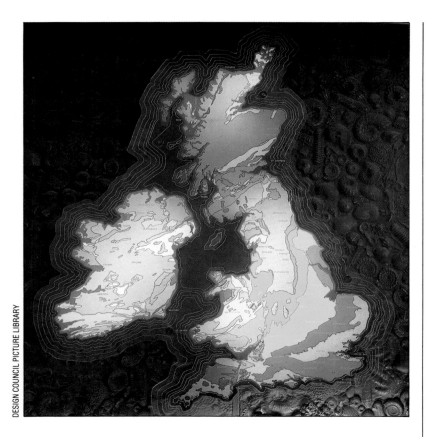

◀ A map specially simplified for exhibition use.

◀ The detail in a commercial map is generally far too fine for use on a panel in an exhibition.

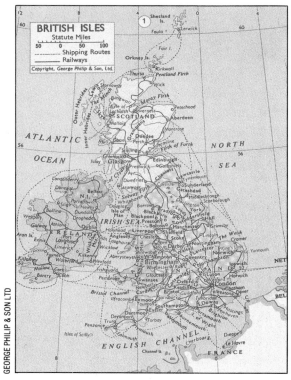

drawn and reproduced using print and details readable at the distances and scales which obtain in the exhibition for which they are planned. Whereas most commercial maps contain a wealth of detail, the exhibition requires only a small proportion of the information available. To obscure the relevant information with these details is unnecessary and bad practice. It must always be remembered that exhibitions are peculiar places in which to receive information — not at all normal. 'Normal' is TV, radio or newspapers and, whereas perhaps half the population of the western world reads a newspaper daily, and nearly all see TV of one sort or another, it is unlikely that half that number of people sees any exhibition in an entire year. The percentages speak for themselves.

Computer Display

Meanwhile, through the TV monitor, computers are playing an ever larger part in the day-to-day lives of the population and these must now be considered to be normal members of the battery of devices available for communicating in exhibitions. While they can contain words and pictures in one form or another, they can also both control working exhibits, and interact with the visitor using either a simplified or normal keyboard. A simplified keyboard can range from a yes/no button to a set of letters and numbers which give access to the information within

► Part of a normally complex computer keyboard which requires some training before use.

►► An immediately understandable, simplified keyboard giving access to the same computer.

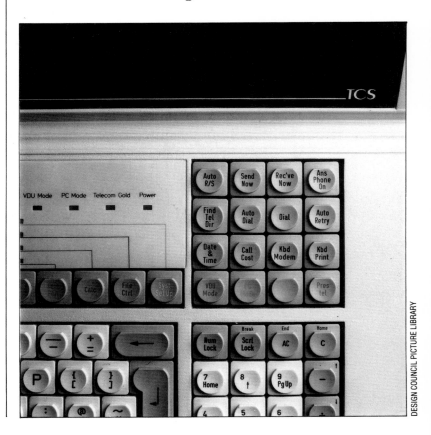

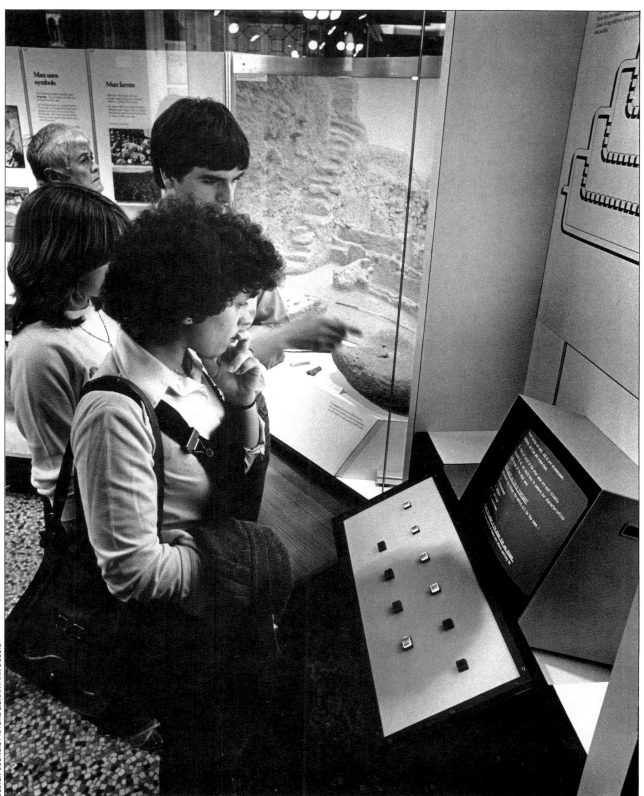

the computer, or separate picture source, slides, video tape or disk. The technology involved is changing almost daily, so any explicit suggestions will undoubtedly go out of date before this book is published. The designer embarking on the use of computers and video-interactive displays should remember, though, that if there is only one available and it seems to be fun, a crowd of unhappy people will rapidly form impatiently awaiting their turn. Therefore such equipment should only be used when a limited number of specialist visitors are expected or if there is money and space to provide a larger number of terminals. Another important factor is the production of suitable program material. This should only be done by experts and, again, the exhibition context should be remembered. Information should be given in short doses of a maximum of two minutes' duration. Long descriptions, needing continuous perusal, are out of the question.

An entire chapter has been devoted to the detailed discussion of words in an exhibition, and their importance cannot be overstated. A number of exhibition designers consider words to be almost irrelevant, while an equal number of exhibitors believe words to be the most important part of a display. In 1985 the Boilerhouse, a specialist design gallery, in the V & A at the time, had an introductory panel containing 2000 words — the equivalent of a sizeable magazine article. It was presumably considered essential reading for the poor visitor on entering the exhibition. Both extremes are of course absurd. A happy balance has to be achieved; objects relative to each other can 'speak' volumes. A sequence of real examples of all stages in the production of a ceramic jug, for instance, will make a fascinating explanatory display with practically no words at all. Similar relative displays can be made under countless circumstances, and any display which allows or encourages the visitor to explore and discover visually rather than literally is exactly suitable for exhibition purposes. Long explanations beg the need for an exhibition at all; perhaps a book would have been better.

Words can be produced in many different ways and, while Chapter 4 dealt with the actual writing of words, followed by their typographic production, there is another way — sound. This divides into three types: general sound where the whole exhibition is addressed, specific sound where only parts of the exhibition contain sound, and individual sound using either handsets, radios or cassette players carried around an exhibition to receive specific information in specific places. Again, the technology for the devices is advancing daily: radio signals or pulses from buried loops, shortwave radio and so on. They are best in the hands of specialist firms that deal with both the production of the programmes and the installation. It is important to remember that with both general and specific sound, noise 'leaks' from the environment for which it was created. Many public and commercial exhibition organisers forbid the use of such equipment, particularly near aisles, as it interferes with neighbouring exhibitors. In an enclosed exhibition, sound can become an irritant so it is again important to use professionals in both its production and projection. The difference between a commentary spoken and produced by amateurs and that done by a professional actor and producer is enormous. The awful, distressed cadences of 'our managing director', when repeated every few minutes, will lose more customers than they will gain. Professionalism, in all subsidiary disciplines in an exhibition, is worth paying for in the long run.

―――――――――― Special Effects ――――――――――

As more and more mention is made of the specialist, we naturally move on to the area of special effects. The whole business of communicating effectively in an exhibition is beset with problems, the greatest of which is keeping the interest of the visitor in probably the most complex circumstances for communicating yet devised. The difficulty is in exploiting continuously the three dimensions in which the communication takes place. As has often been stated, the only reason for the exhibition is that 'space' is needed and, once involved in space, it is pointless to fill it up simply with words to form what in the trade are ridiculed as 'books on legs'. It is far easier to read sitting at home or in the

▼ 'A book on legs', the designer's nickname for an exhibition vastly overstocked with text.

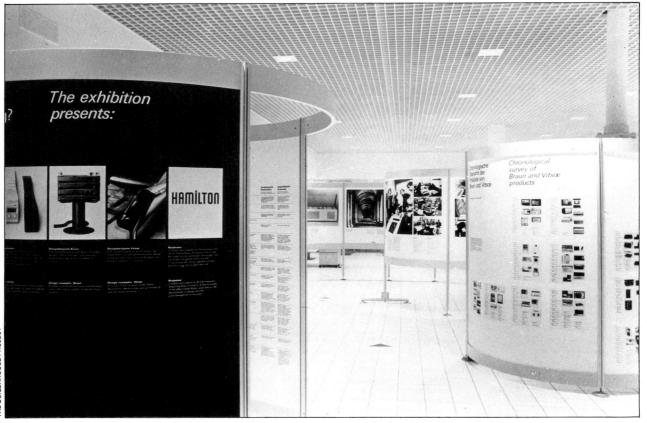

THE BOILERHOUSE PROJECT

office, and if literature is needed to accompany an exhibition, that is where it will eventually either be read, or passed over. All special effects are expensive, however, so careful consideration must be given to the suitability of the effect in the circumstances of the information.

To deal with space in the most effective way, various techniques have evolved and will of course go on evolving. One of the earliest display techniques to emerge was the diorama. This is a modelled painting. Fake perspectives are cleverly exploited in shallow depth to give the impression of great depth. The whole effect is carefully modelled and realistically painted and set up, often using real objects in the foreground. When well lit and carefully sited, they give an impression of reality frozen in time. These models can vary from life size down to really very small with perhaps a viewing aperture of only half a square metre. But the effect of depth and therefore reality greatly enhances what would otherwise be a dull and formal painting.

A working diorama in particular can have its place in an exhibition. This is a diorama in which the more realistically modelled foreground is made to work or operate in some way, while the accurately perspectived background remains static. It can also be

▼ An enthralling diorama, the 'Great Fire of London' at the Museum of London.

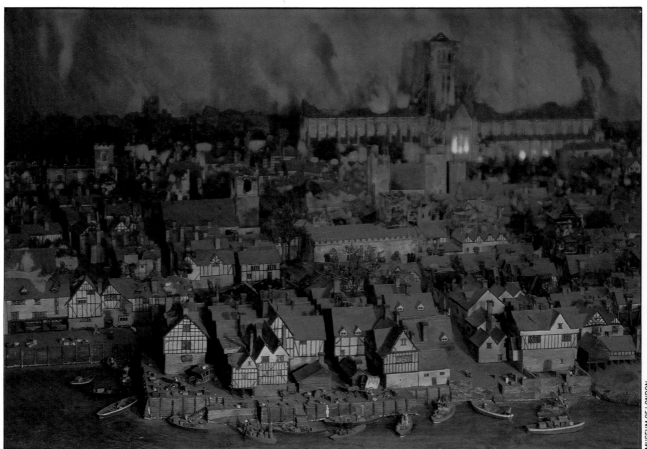

MUSEUM OF LONDON

a drama in which lights or sequenced lighting effects are used to tell a story. The 'Great Fire of London' in the Museum of London is a famous example where a commentary, sound and light effects create a miniature theatre. For a few minutes it is possible to get some sense of reality of the Great Fire and 'what it was like at the time'. The viewing angles and viewing distances are important when considering dioramas of any kind; the specialist commissioned to make one should see the actual venue, or at least accurate, detailed drawings of it before commencing work. It should also be decided whether the diorama is to be oriented towards adults or children, or both, as with narrow viewing angles and a small diorama it can be difficult to get people in the right place for the best possible view. Some, particularly landscapes, are best seen at first from a distance, whereas working dioramas with complex effects probably demand a close view. Remember that adults can always bend, but children cannot suddenly grow 450 mm unless steps are provided. Even then, if steps of the wrong height are provided, children will simply block the view of the adults.

Another old technique is the Pepper's Ghost, named after John H. Pepper (1821–1900) who perfected H. Dircks's invention for

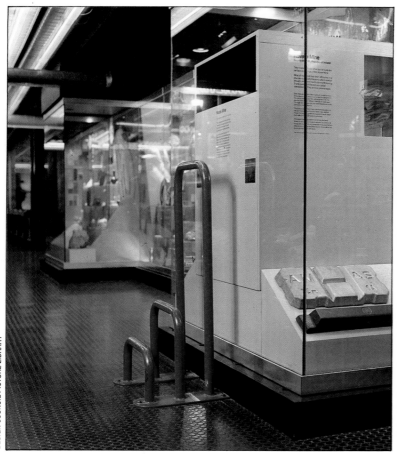

◄ **This display has a very specific viewing position – simple steps make it possible for everybody to see it. 'Treasures of the Earth', Geological Museum, 1985.**

melodramas on the Victorian stage. A Pepper's Ghost exploits the quality of glass that allows it to be at its most transparent when there is a bright light beyond it, and at its most reflective when there is darkness beyond it. Thus, by adjusting lights and the angle of the glass, it is possible to create the effect of one three-dimensional image replacing another image before the eyes of the visitor. By careful interplay of lights, angles, real and reflected images, it is possible also to create the effect of a 'ghost' where one image is 'floated' over another. The effect is contrived by the use of semi-silvered glass; that is glass which is half obscured by fine silvering.

For the technically minded, the effect is achieved by a bright light shining on the real image beyond the glass to give a sharp image, while another bright light is faded up or down on to the reflected image. The semi-silvering makes the reflected image quite as sharp as the real image, particularly with the silvered side of the glass closest to the viewer. When the balance of light is totally reversed, so that all light is on the reflected image, the real image completely disappears. Even more so than with dioramas, the viewing angles are important — in this case critical — and the exact matching of the two images is a job requiring great skill and meticulous modelling. Pepper's Ghosts can be used, therefore, for showing 'before and after' situations or for showing

▼ ▶ On pressing the button the workings of this mine are slowly superimposed over the body of ore underground. 'Treasures of the Earth', Geological Museum, 1985.

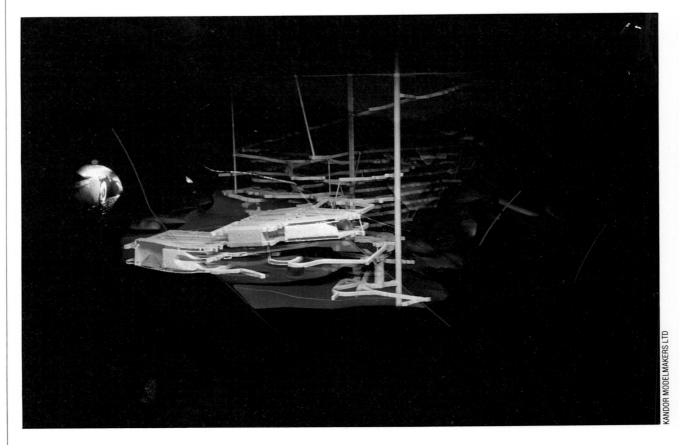

KANDOR MODELMAKERS LTD

two distinct aspects of a complex structure such as the ore body in a mine with a superimposition of the mining shafts and tunnels. Another use, for example, is where an object on display is 'ghosted' in and out of view to be replaced by pictures and text related to it.

There are countless uses for these special effects and, once the imaginative designer has got hold of a new technique, it will undoubtedly be developed further. One such development arose from the need to show a possible career path to teenage visitors. A simple mirror confronted the visitor with the suggestion that he should press a button to plan the path of his career; immediately the button was pressed, a pattern of lines emerged over his reflection in the mirror, showing a likely career pattern. This was done simply by using a semi-silvered mirror as the front glass in a transparency, and shining a strong light on the visitor. When the button was pressed, the strong light was dimmed and the transparency illuminated from behind. Again, viewing angles and positions have to be examined. Models, dioramas and Pepper's Ghosts can be mixed with both front and back projections from slide or film material. Completely white relief models can be made, upon which coloured data is projected — even for subjects as complex as maps. Translucent models can be made. Glass-reinforced plastic (GRP) is translucent, for example, where

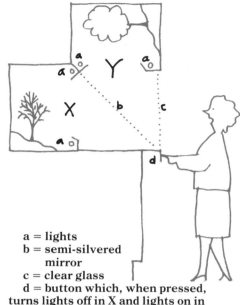

a = lights
b = semi-silvered
    mirror
c = clear glass
d = button which, when pressed, turns lights off in X and lights on in Y. If pressed again it reverses the process. The tree can be seen with or without leaves. The lights can also be faded up and down.

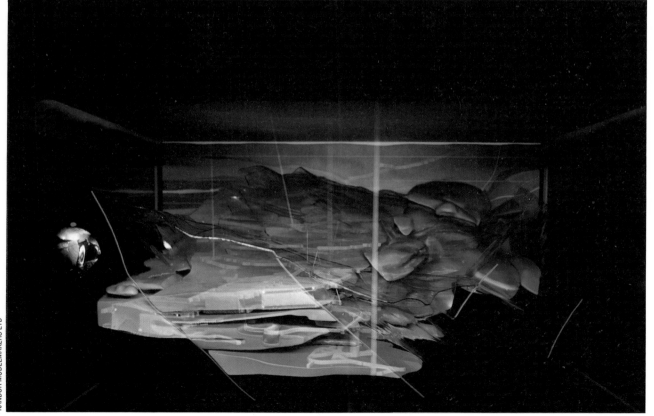

one set of information is apparent when the model is back-lit and another when it is front-lit. The final stage in a diorama, the flat artwork at the rear, can be back projected and then changed, using cross-fade slides or film. Changing or running titles can be introduced. Planned, computer-controlled sequences can be used and operated by the visitor. The permutations are endless.

Semi-silvered mirror has been discussed at length, but ordinary mirror has a great part to play in the exhibition environment. It can be used to enlarge a seemingly narrow space. By placing mirrors strategically they can create an effect of spaciousness and continuance where none exists. Used in models, they can have the same effect; half-ship models, where a mirror reflects the other half, used to be commonplace. An enclosed landscape model will look 'boxed in', but when slim mirrors are placed at each end the model will seem to continue, again giving a feeling of length where none exists. They can be used on ceilings, subject to safety regulations (mirror plastic is available), to give an impression of height; on structures to give the impression that the supported load floats; and on floors, adequately protected by subtle barriers, to give the effect that a column or tower grows out from below the floor. They can be used under water, behind flowers, beside curtains, at the back of recesses. Mirrors used in these ways, decoratively but with practical considerations or illusion in mind, are again an area where the designer's ingenuity will always find new uses. This book cannot teach people how to

▶ Topography and geology are projected from overhead on to the white relief map. 'Britain before Man', Geological Museum, 1977.

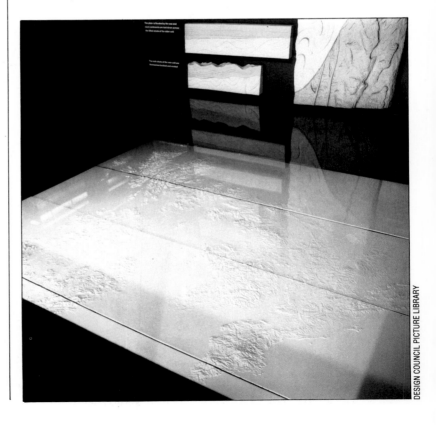

design; all it can do is to open doors to solutions to design problems. Mirrors used completely for practical purposes also have a place. Where distances immediately behind a rear projection screen are too confined, the projected beam can be lengthened by the use of front silvered mirrors, but remember that every time the image passes through a mirror, it is reversed and somewhat degraded.

There are one or two other special effects that come into this area of solid or quasi-solid images. The first is a development of polaroid, where the qualities of polaroid film are exploited to produce moiré patterns which simulate movement on flat diagrams. Discs of polaroid are revolved behind static cut-out polaroid patterns, set into black and white on coloured film. With a light source behind them, an effect is produced where, for example, a diagram showing the flow of fuel through an engine, the fuel seems to flow. Another patented device is the 'talking head'. This is, in the writer's opinion, a sinister device, best only for demonstrations in the Chamber of Horrors. A completely static mask is sculpted in white relief and on to it is projected generally a well-known person explaining some phenomenon or other. As the relief model is completely static, and as the talker's head has to be held in a clamp during filming, the result is macabre in the extreme, but it does seem to generate a delighted response from the very young. Another patented device, which should be popular only with the young but seems to appeal also to those of us

▼ **Back-lit polaroid discs and film are moved against each other to produce the effect of movement in a flat display. © Technical Animations Ltd.**

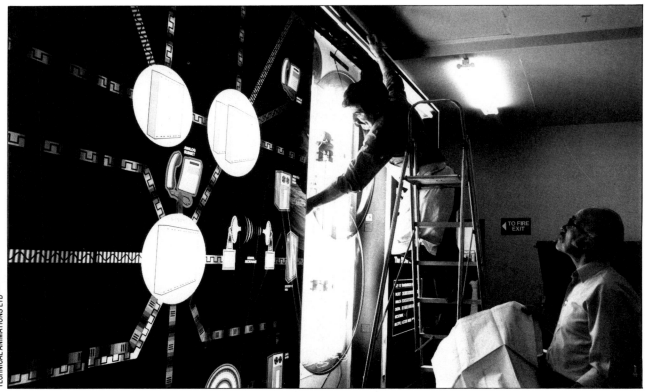

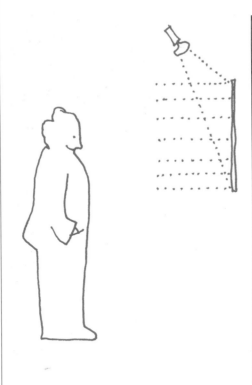

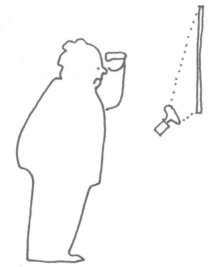

▲ A hologram must be lit from the same angle from which it was lit when photographed . . .

. . . if it isn't, it is simply invisible.

who like practical jokes, is a televised animated cartoon face, which calls out to the passers-by and engages them in conversation. There is a large group of people, of whom the writer is one, who would run a mile rather than talk to a televised cartoon, but surprisingly others exist who quite cheerfully do so. The device consists of a manually manipulated rubber drawing, which can be made to perform a number of basic facial movements. It is manipulated by an operator with a microphone, who is concealed behind a one-way transparent screen. The eventual image is videoed on to a screen.

Finally, and as yet a long way from full development in terms of informative devices, come holograms. To date they have mainly been used as exhibits in their own right, rather than as informative aids. However, holograms responding to low-voltage lighting can be switched off to be transparent and invisible, allowing a further image to be seen beyond. At the time of writing a hologram can only be made by special photography and it is invariably static, but it is likely that it will eventually develop to be both mobile and computer generated. A hologram is a clearly three-dimensional image, contained in a flat plane. It is made by splitting a pure beam of laser light from one source to give both a front and an angled view of an object at the same time, thus creating the impression of depth.

Projection

Projection has already been mentioned in connection with dioramas and working models, but in fact it has a far greater potential role in exhibitions. We are at a point in time where one system of projection looks like taking over from another. Until recently, all projection in exhibitions, either of stills or moving images, has been achieved using conventional methods; that is, a bright light through translucent film. The major attendant problems with this method are two-fold. The lamps burn out and the films fade, so for any exhibition the costs are high and the danger of blank information spaces imminent. Over the last few years, major museums and exhibitions have replaced the ubiquitous slide screen with television monitors showing video tapes. Conferences and major sporting events have called for the development of bigger and better television projection equipment and, in recent years, the development of the video disc as opposed to the video tape has produced a far more refined moving image and a really first-class still picture. As with all new developments, costs at the time of writing are comparatively high, particularly bearing in mind the cost of producing a special disc, but it is likely that with the advance of the technology prices will gently fall and discs with less capacity will be developed for special purposes. Meanwhile, for the ordinary exhibitor, slides with automatic changing lamps and random access, and film loops stored in loop absorbers and projecting continuously will remain useful.

While television projection is undoubtedly in its infancy, normal projection is very sophisticated indeed. The quality of the image

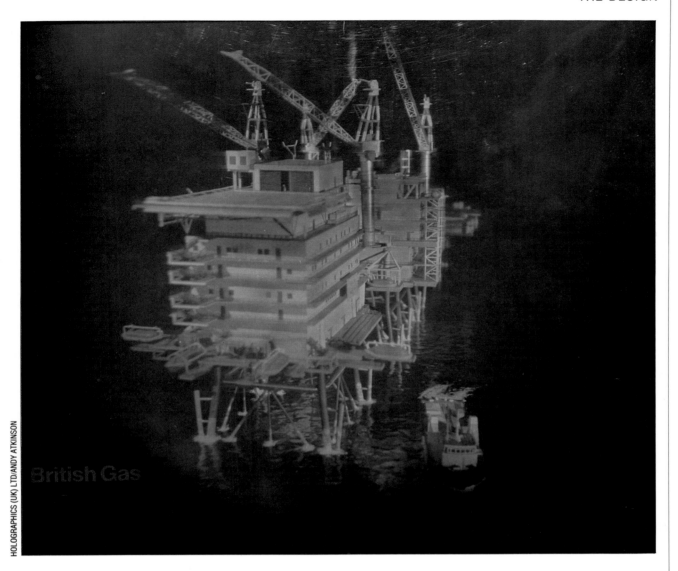

HOLOGRAPHICS (UK) LTD/ANDY ATKINSON

is near-perfect and can be projected on to practically anything. The major controlling factor is the ambient light. Daylight is the arch-enemy of the exhibition designer; it is almost completely impossible to predict and to control satisfactorily if allowed in. The best place for it is out, so where complex projections and lighting effects are required, it is vital to exclude daylight as much as possible. Assuming it is largely excluded, fascinating effects can be produced by projecting on to gauze, pierced screens, leaves, smoke, water (milk has even be used) — almost anything you care to consider. Projection on to gauze can produce ghost effects by filming against black and mixing light levels beyond the gauze with projection on the gauze. Multiscreen projection can be set up where specially prepared programmes accompanied by sound commentaries are shown. These programmes, commonly known as A/V (audio-visual) slide shows are controlled by either

▲ Rainbow/Benton transmission hologram, commissioned by British Gas for the British Gas flotation.

solid state computers or pulsed tape, and have a whole industry devoted to their production. Both the hardware and the software are used for conferences and sales promotions of one sort or another. Some of the slide shows are so sophisticatedly pulsed and cross-faced that they can produce the effect of movement. Split screen projection, where two or more moving images, or a still and moving image mix, are shown is another development.

All these projections must be produced by professionals with expert knowledge. They are costly and, in an exhibition, should be shown for short, clearly stated periods — between one and eight minutes, depending on the comfort of the environment. Eight minutes is a very long time to stand watching a programme. Moreover, they should be used only in short-term exhibitions unless firm maintenance arrangements have been made. Shows using up to 40 projectors leave a great deal to go wrong.

Another simple projection is the tracking panorama, where a filmed 'mural' is passed slowly before the viewer with an accompanying sound track. It is complex to achieve, but not expensive, and when done with skill is most effective. At the time of writing, the most durable method of slowly changing or moving images is undoubtedly television, but in its simplest form — a television monitor — it is very restricting and in its most complex form — projection — it is expensive. Durability is vital; there is nothing worse in an exhibition than a blank space where an image is supposed to be, and an impatient audience waiting for it.

Sound It has been impossible to write thus far without the mention of sound and it is, of course, commonplace with all sorts of projection, but it is worth considering on its own. Not all sound has to be spoken commentary. Sound effects can enhance a simple display: the sound of birds with an outdoor effect on diorama, or wind and seagulls with ships or coastal scenes. It may sound corny, and indeed it is, but corn sells a lot of products and is equally useful in selling information. Sound can be more or less localised, using directional speakers, but often a discreet spill of sound lends atmosphere and acts as an enticement to visitors to move nearer to the source. Handset telephone receivers can be used, though they are vulnerable to vandals, and a recent development is solid state sound — another area of rapid advance in technology — where up to nine minutes on three separate tracks can be stored and transmitted without the use of tape, and will start at the beginning for every new visitor pulsing his presence. Sound, like all the other specialities, is best in the hands of experts, but the designer should keep up to date with the potentials from all effects in order to communicate effectively.

Having considered sound, smell should not be forgotten. Atmosphere has often been mentioned as conducive to learning in these peculiar environments, and smell can be used discreetly to great effect. Many smells are very evocative and can be

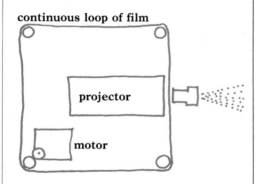

continuous loop of film

projector

motor

▲ **A tracking panorama. A loop of film taken by a mapping camera is passed in front of a simple projector along with a synchronised soundtrack if required.**

reproduced synthetically. A pressure pad-operated gas cylinder producing, at nose level, a shot of an appropriate odour at a good moment, can be a marvellous gimmick; gimmicks are after all what most of the effects are, and why not, if they assist in the process of enlightenment?

────────────────── Lighting ──────────────────

Light itself is the final piece in the jigsaw puzzle of special effects. It is a puzzle, however, that can be rearranged in countless ways. The only way to bring order to the description of the pieces has been to separate them, but there are inevitably hundreds of different permutations awaiting invention. Light is clearly the most important of all the elements relative to effective display. It is the one thing that cannot be removed. At the same time it is possible to use it poorly and inadequately, particularly as it seems to be the area in which the least startling developments have taken place since the late 1960s. Sources of light have been honed down and become more sophisticated but they still boil down to two, generally referred to as tungsten and fluorescent (in other words, a hot bulb or a cool tube). Tungsten lamps have been tidied up and low voltage devices developed; fluorescent tubes have been slimmed down and bent into shapes resembling light bulbs, but we are still stuck with the same two basic forms. It is, as yet, not possible to paint on light or to bend it, or to float it in space, or to pulse shots of it along transparent tubes. We delight in laser shows but find it very hard to use lasers economically for display. Light awaits its 'Silicon Valley'.

Meanwhile, what have we got? Tungsten and all its derivatives, halogen, quartz and so on, all giving varying degrees of sharp, hot light with a warm effect with which, even though it is not a 'natural' light and is hard to filter into one, we are most at ease. People choose tungsten generally for living rooms, for instance. In its simplest form it is used in the ordinary 25, 40, 60 and 100 watt bulbs, but exhibitions are not normally about exhibiting lamps and lampshades. They are about using lamps effectively and not much joy can be got out of a 40-watt bulb. Essentially, the general internal lighting of a display should be recessive and its external lighting, titling and so on should be competitive. Internally, the lighting of the displays should be paramount and frequently in an introverted exhibition the displays will emanate enough light to illuminate the exhibition, with the possible assistance of discreet handrail, skirting or cornice lighting to define the public spaces. Fluorescent tubes are ideal for such linear lighting, along with the even lighting of fascias or transparencies and the front-lighting of dioramas and models. Tungsten light is physically hot, easy to control, throws sharp shadows and can be projected over long distances. Fluorescent light is cool, comparatively hard to control, fade or turn on or off without special equipment and throws vague, fuzzy shadows. Essentially when light is used for display, it should be used profusely and internally, but economically. Profusely means that there should be plenty of light. Displays ought to

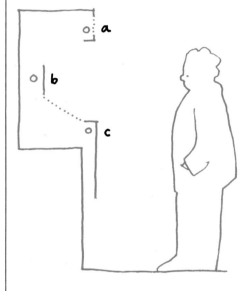

a = striplight lighting the display and back lighting a fret-cut fascia
b = striplight lighting up and down and through a transparency
c = striplight lighting the display and a skirting recess.

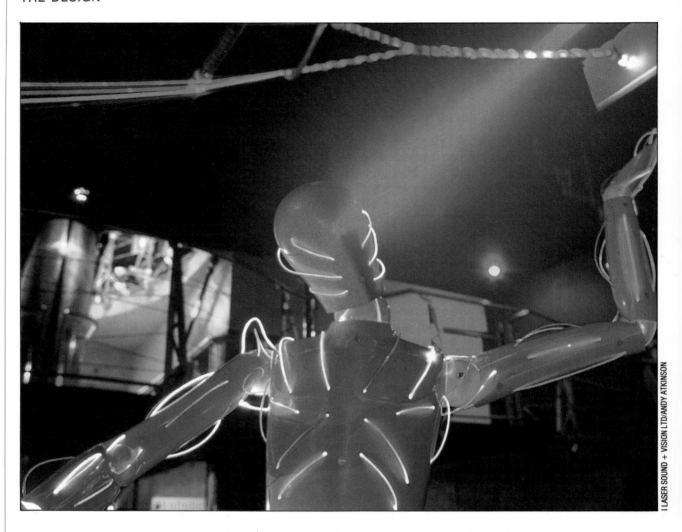

I LASER SOUND + VISION LTD/ANDY ATKINSON

▲ **Laser light passed through glass fibres produces this dramatic effect.**

twinkle and cry out for attention. Internally means that the lamps should be within the confines of the display. If they are outside, they will cast shadows and cause reflections in display case glass. Economically means that as much value should be got out of each lamp as possible. Both tungsten and fluorescent lamps cause problems for conservationists, when used near valuable fabrics, paintings or prints. They both produce heat, albeit in differing quantities, but more importantly they produce light. It is high numbers of lumens — measured light — that do the damage. Consult conservators before lighting precious artefacts and consult lighting experts before embarking on extensive lighting systems.

There are other, less common, sources of light. We are all familiar with neon and it is in fact very usable. It is the only source of light with which it is possible to draw, albeit with stylised lines, and it can be pulsed on and off easily; hence the exotic advertisements for which it is used. It is, however, dangerous stuff when used at very high voltages even when

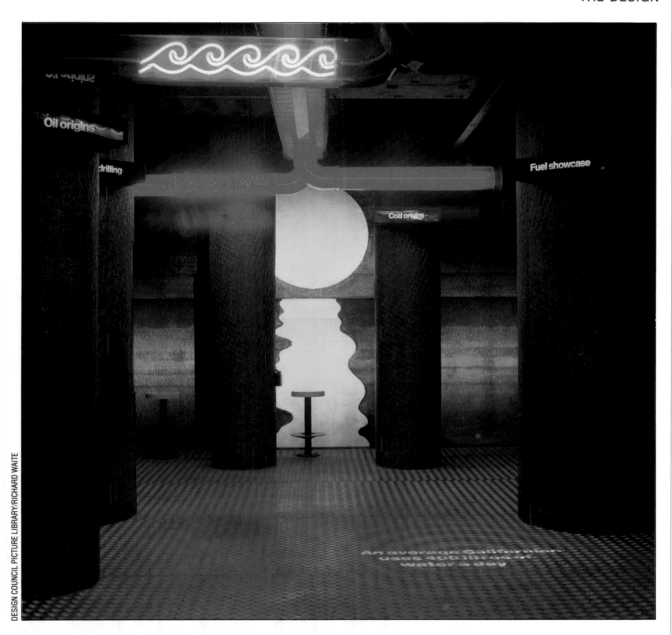

▲ Neon used for fascia symbols in 'Treasures of the Earth', Geological Museum, 1985.

designed properly within legal constraints. It can only be manufactured to order and installed by experts, but it can be an excellent solution to certain problems, particularly as it can be made in a surprisingly wide range of colours using permutations: different gases and coloured tubes. Lasers are another light source, as yet only played with for exhibition purposes. No doubt useful developments will emerge as a by-product of some other more sophisticated, often military, requirement.

Other ways of transmitting light have been developed in recent years, one or two of them useful to the exhibition designer. Fibre optics, glass or plastics fibres will transmit sharp, bright light to tiny outlets some distance away from the source. This can be most useful in tiny or interactive displays. In edge lighting, the molecular structure of Perspex sheets allows light put in at one edge of a sheet of Perspex to be emitted, either on an engraved line, or at the other end of the sheet. Thus engraved drawings can be illuminated dramatically.

Perhaps the most magic source of light of them all is ultraviolet (U/V), or black light, which can be used to transmit light invisibly across a space. There are U/V sensitive paints, plastics (and soap powders), which respond dramatically to remote black light and provide almost a neon-like effect, but the light is not bright, so it needs to be in a subdued ambiance.

All these types of light and effects can and should interplay with other aspects of a display to produce really exciting results.

Interactive Displays

Special effects are subject to two main types of operation; either automatic or interactive. The first means operating continuously and

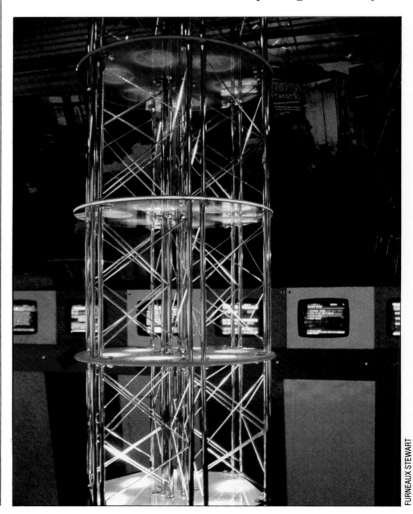

► Use of Perspex in an exhibition: Furneaux Stewart's design for British Telecom's stand at the 1983 Ideal Home Exhibition.

►► An interactive display in 'Man's Place in Evolution', British Museum (Natural History), 1980.

FURNEAUX STEWART

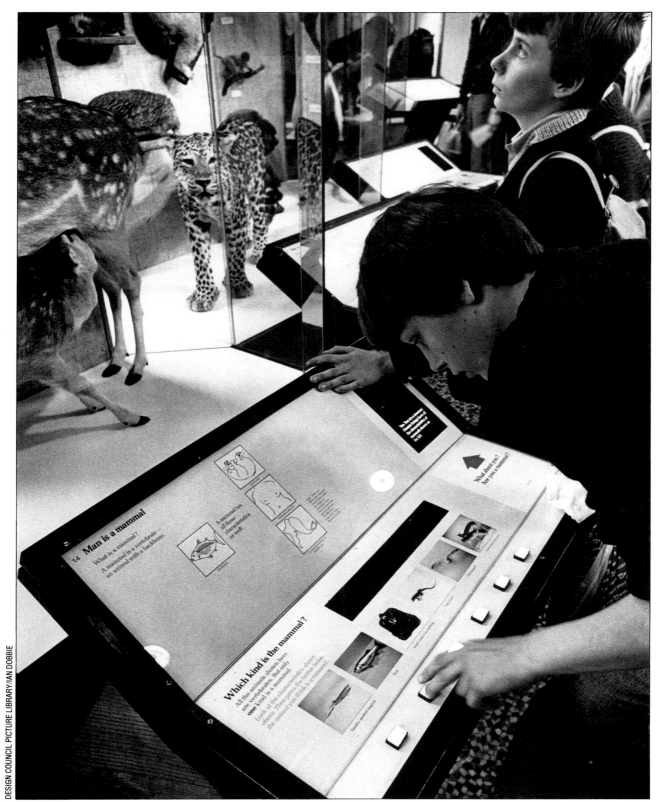

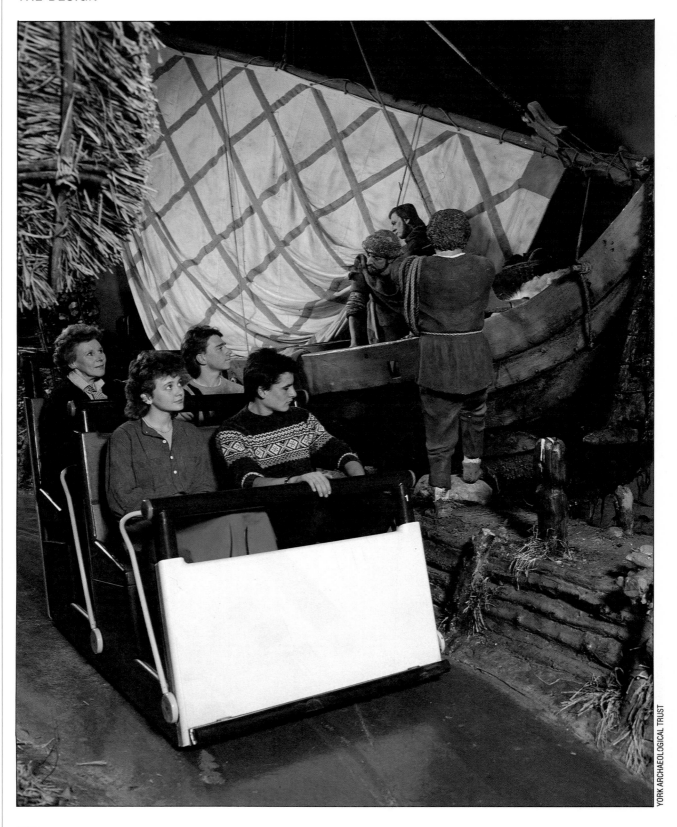

sequentially; the second means operated by the visitor, individually or because of his or her arrival at the display. Automatic displays are easy and straightforward, but interactive displays give the visitor the chance to explore independently, and they are greatly favoured in science or education-oriented displays in museums or interpretative centres. In these situations, the visitor's interest is generated by the display and further interest encouraged through visitor involvement. A display that responds to the visitor's arrival, participation and departure will obviously generate greater interest and, despite the sophistication of its working parts, can be of enormous value in communicating.

If the visitor is to operate an exhibit, then various methods have to be considered. There are not only buttons to press. The adjoining button is useful, though commonplace. Other impulses used are hidden; weight-sensitive pressure pads, placed underneath carpeting, respond to the visitor's presence or arrival and initiate a response, or set of responses. There are also ultrasonic switches and radar controlled switches. Sound and heat sensitive switches also exist and, again, we are in the area of advancing technology, so further discussion of types of switches is irrelevant except to say that if buttons are to be used they must of course be tough and durable. The type of 'magic' response to the visitor's arrival provided by impulse methods is exactly the stuff of successful exhibitions and, when used imaginatively, can enhance the process of three-dimensional learning immensely.

Finally, the ultimate (to date) special effect: travel — the automated travel of the visitor through the exhibition, or of the exhibition past the visitor. This involves using cars on tracks, buried cables, or giant revolves, all highly complex and expensive methods and only to be considered where there is money and expertise enough to develop the techniques, for there is no 'standard' model. There are examples of these in the western world, and before the exhibitor or designer embarks upon this way of exhibiting, it would be as well to visit such exhibitions, to find out the benefits, snags and costs. Such movement can be dramatic, exciting and fun, and when information is merged with such qualities there is a strong chance that the communication will be effective. That of course is what the design is all about.

But creativity cannot be taught. All this chapter has done has been to present most of the elements which can be part of a good design. It is up to the imagination of the designer to mix some, or all, of these elements effectively.

◄ **Electric cars transport the visitor through the popular part of the Jorvik Viking exhibition in ten minutes. The visitors then walk through the more didactic part of the exhibition at their own pace.**

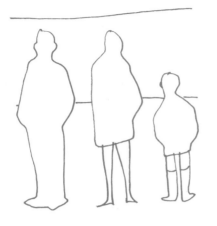

Do remember people's eyesight varies.
Remember

bifocals

short-sighted people

short people

tall people

disabled people

people who want to touch things.

Do remember people have noses and ears as well as eyes.

Do remember people have needs

to sit down

to quench their thirst

to go to the toilet

to hang up their coats

to protect their valuables.

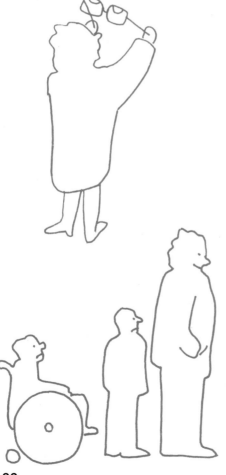

Do remember some people want

to destroy things

to blow things up

to steal things.

Do respect existing buildings.

. . . AND DON'T'S

Do not create attractive exhibits full of interest and detail that block the entrance and exit points of the exhibition.

Do not place detailed displays in such a way that a visitor looking at them will obscure other displays.

Do not design tall detailed displays. One visitor can obscure the whole thing. Orient displays laterally.

Do not put detailed information outside a band 900 mm from the floor to 2000 mm from the floor. Nobody will read it.

Do not put lights where they will blind visitors the other side of the display.

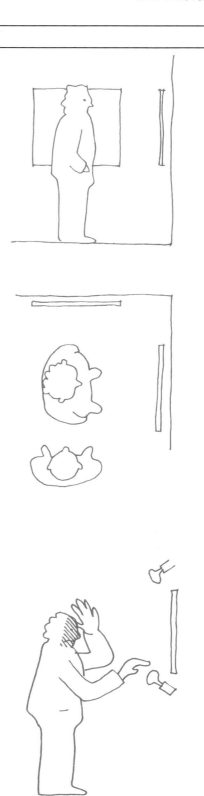

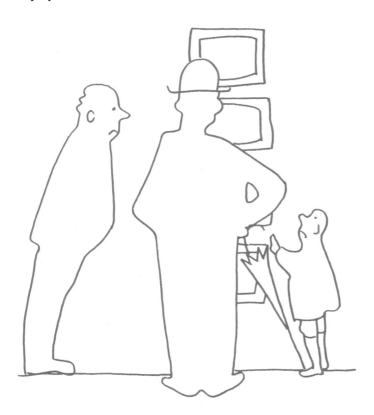

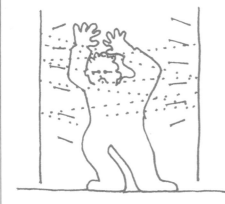

Do not put showcases with vertical glass opposite each other; this will create a hall of mirrors.

Do not force or expect people to follow a compulsory route. They will not.

Do not use long line lengths: 40 to 50 characters maximum.

Do not label deep cases with small print front and back. Choose one that can be read all over.

Do not site good displays in out of the way places.

Do not put labels to pictures in the shadow below them.

Do not use handwriting.

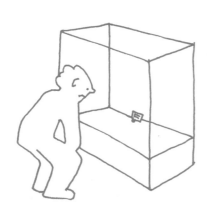

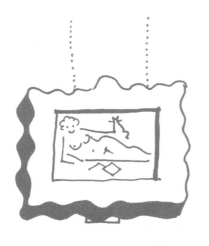

What is Taste?

Taste is one of the processes we use to make judgements about design.

The body of information we draw upon in making these judgements has accumulated across the centuries. This exhibition aims to show how this accumulation took place.

But the process is not finite: it continues today. Humans have traditional purposes and evolving needs: the process of Taste has to serve both.

The present moment is one of great diversity in matters of Taste. In revealing some of the important influences in the history of Taste this exhibition is intended to help us understand more clearly why we value certain values in design; if we can know what influences us today then perhaps we can more effectively decide what we want tomorrow.

The concept of Taste evolved when at one moment in the past there was such diversity that it was necessary to make a clear statement about what constituted the "good" in design. "Good" design and "good" taste are not necessarily the same thing: Taste is not the whole of design because it ignores function and finance, but it is the most human, immediate and evocative part of it. An exhibition about Taste is an exhibition about _values_ in design ...

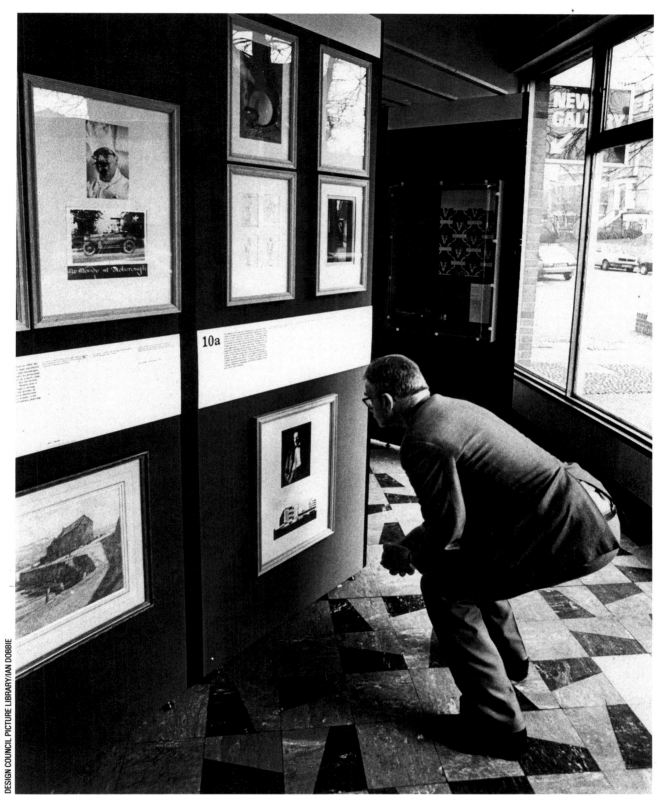

6
THE MANAGEMENT

Any enterprise involving more than one person has to be managed; even lifting a plank can be hazardous if there is no co-ordination. If the plank has to be made, purchased, delivered, used and eventually disposed of within an ordained sum of money and period of time, then clearly a certain amount of expertise is required. Needless to say, even the simplest exhibition is a little more complex than a plank. Professional management is therefore essential if it is to be executed successfully. A designer must appreciate the need for management as a separate field of expertise, even if he or she is a 'good manager'. If this is not appreciated, and the designer attempts to manage as well as design the project, time-consuming details will distract attention from the considerable demands of design already discussed.

Management should not be considered a lesser profession than design; it is simply a different one. There is no reason why a good, senior exhibition design manager should not head up a production team — in fact it can be as well if one does, using management skills to shield the creative part of the team in order to get the best out of it. Good management is a smooth, efficient, creative process adding enormously to the value of the end product; good exhibition design managers are hard to come by, largely because there is no specific training for them.

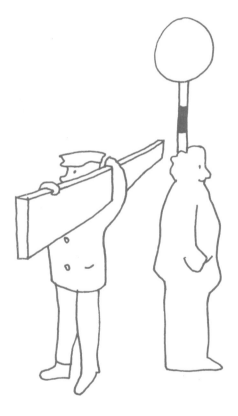

The best background for a manager is probably contractual. The successful manager might well have spent some early years in an exhibition or shopfitting works, moving from section to section learning the processes involved, or from one contracting firm to another, seeking experience and advancement. Early days might have been spent as a tea-boy, carpenter's mate, management trainee, draughtsperson or an apprentice estimator. No matter what, production experience and a fair, if general, grounding in costing and financial matters along with contracts, transport and site work is fundamental.

If a student on a design course shows a weakness in creative skills but organisational strengths, then management might well be a good course for that person to follow after graduation. Junior work in a design office, with a strong emphasis on management and production problems could make a good basis upon which to build a management career. It must be emphasised however that, while exhibition management is without specialist training, general management skills can be taught and there are many specialist degree, post-graduate and diploma courses. Such training, combined with reasonable practical experience in the exhibition industry, could well produce a very effective manager.

There is a practical side to most designers' work which should enable a designer to appreciate the need for management and organisation. This chapter is devoted to describing aspects of good management which will hopefully assist in the relationship between design and management, with the aim of producing first-rate large or small exhibitions.

MANAGERIAL QUALITIES

The ideal manager will be flexible, outgoing, gregarious and able to relate equally to suppliers, designers and contractors and to command their respect. He or she must not be easily manipulated — and will need to be tough but good-mannered. An understanding of the need for production and financial control and constraints is essential, as is respect for and understanding of designers and the need for design.

We should nod in the direction of overseas exhibitions at this point. They fall into two general categories; those planned in the home country and constructed abroad, and those planned and constructed in the home country and erected by home contractors on a foreign site. The former should really only apply to the simplest possible constructions such as shell schemes; there are too many accidents possible if there is anything complex involved. Not all countries have the same or similar organisations for exhibition production, so if any foreign venture is envisaged then a preliminary visit is essential to establish lines of communication. In the second category, shipping clearly becomes a major consideration, weight and size obviously affecting cost, and shipping time obviously affecting any production schedule. There are professional shipping agencies in most countries, and they should be consulted at the outset. There can also be problems with foreign labour on foreign soil. These vary from country to country, and embassy officials (commercial attachés) ought to know the answers, and ought to be consulted.

Because management is essential, chronological and procedural, it is best to present the management involvement in the form of a production chart. This will evolve through phases over the next few pages. Phases have been chosen to allow for different scales of operation to be dealt with. Because this chapter is about management, that aspect of exhibitions is placed at the top of the chart. Normally such a chart would show the critical path of design and production in the primary position, with the necessary procedures below. The client's role is necessarily small, for he has, after all, paid to have it all done. The phases allow for different time scales for projects, categorised as follows:

Major projects International world fairs, festivals, such as the National Garden Festivals in Liverpool, Stoke-on-Trent or Glasgow. Galleries or whole new museums, for instance, the Quai d'Orsay in Paris, large permanent national museum galleries, either science or fine art oriented. Whole new heritage or eco-centres.

Large projects Temporary exhibitions such as motor shows or boat shows. Central features such as those at the Boat Show or Ideal Home Exhibition. Large, temporary national museum exhibitions. Permanent galleries in major provincial museums. Environment, heritage or eco-centres.

Medium projects Whole shell schemes or stands at trade fairs or specialist exhibitions such as computer, electronics, business, or heating and ventilating exhibitions. One-off special exhibitions organised in association with major conferences. Small permanent galleries in provincial museums, the temporary but complex exhibitions in national museums. Large portable or travelling exhibitions.

Small projects Portable, 'suitcase' displays. Foyer or library displays. Window displays — normally done by specialists, but occasionally mounted by companies or museums when the odd window becomes available.

These categories can only serve as a rough guide. There is room for great variety within them; therefore the timing allocated to each phase must be looked at with a certain amount of circumspection — they are to help, not to instruct. The most important thing is to relate the procedural stage with the production activity, for it is the responsibility of the manager to define this in consultation with the designer and client, and then to ensure that each deadline is met. At the time of writing there are microcomputer programs available, associated with the building trade, which can collate all the production activities with personnel and finance. Similar programs for exhibition production would be of enormous value.

Exhibitions in the commercial field *have* to open on time; exhibitions or new galleries in museums can open when they are ready. This is very poor practice, for without the stimulus of deadline it is likely that they would never open at all. Hence the need for the biggest VIP who can be found to stimulate activity.

The following chart, drawn up with the help of an experienced manager, indicates in broad terms the roles and responsibilities of the manager, client and designer in the schedule leading up to opening day of the exhibition.

PHASE 1

CATEGORY	WEEKS
Major	105
Large	20
Medium	12
Small	8

Management
Senior, with project manager

- Project manager receives and arranges budget allocation.
- Schedules projected to produce critical path. Co-ordinates arrangement and disperal of responsibilities with project designer.

Management team
One manager

- Makes approaches to VIP etc for opening.

Client
Senior, with project delegate

- Ratifies budget allocation and clears funding, bill-paying procedures etc.

Design
Senior, with project designer, team leader, single designer.
Later: graphic designer

- Agrees budget, schedules and allocations of responsibilities.
- Works on brief with creative team, scriptwriter particularly, to produce draft script/story board and sketch treatments.
- Architects and engineers to be consulted if necessary.

PHASE 2

CATEGORY	WEEKS
Major	100
Large	18
Medium	11
Small	7

Management

- Accurate budget forecasts for site hire, construction, typesetting, electrics and special effects.
- Deadline date fixed, critical path established.
- Responsibilities co-ordinated. Client liaison and reassurance.

Client

- Client approval initialled.

Design

- Overall design completed, models or visuals produced with suggestions of graphic treatment.
- Titles and sub-titles established.
- Researched script ready for presentation.

PHASE 3

CATEGORY	WEEKS
Major	90
Large	16
Medium	9
Small	6

Management
- Co-ordination of competitive tendering. Single tender action in hand. Contracts drawn up, agreed and finalised.
- Penalty clauses, deadlines confirmed to contractor.
- VIPs confirmed.

Client
- Check and revise if necessary.
- Final signed agreement to all proposals.

Design
- Working drawings completed and printed for tendering.
- Special effects decided and briefs prepared for commissions.
- Decisions with main contractor and special effects contractors.
- Text finalised. Graphic design type mock-ups in hand with typesetter.

PHASE 4

CATEGORY	WEEKS
Major	80
Large	14
Medium	8
Small	5

Management
- Translators arranged.
- Ongoing budget control and supervision. Finalised authorisation of payments etc.
- Acquisition of exhibits – hire and loan.
- Insurance and indemnities. Progress chasing.

Client
- Ongoing overview – proof-reading etc.
- Stand staff planning; literature and stand supplies.
- Drink and food ordered.

Design
- General supervision of graphics. Attention to detail of mounting special effects.
- Supervision of contractors in workshops; visits etc.
- Graphic designer to finalise illustrations, graphs, charts, photographs etc. Supervision.
- Guides for cut-out letters, signwriting etc.

PHASE 5	
CATEGORY	WEEKS
Major	70
Large	12
Medium	6
Small	4

Management
- Liaison with client on production of support literature, brochures, posters etc. Booking of hotels, air, road and rail transport; shipping agents. Customs.
- Liaison with organisers, building supervisors, fire and safety officers. Schedule chasing.
- Visits with designers to special-effects and main contractors.

Client
- Liaison with management over ancillary details as above.

Design
- Liaison and supervision of special-effects and electrical contractors. Day-by-day contact with management re timing and finance and possible further or lesser expenditure on various items.
- Graphic designer preparing finished art work, photographs.
- Liaison with specialist producers, screen printers, colour processors. Photographic and A/V pictures.

PHASE 6	
CATEGORY	WEEKS
Major	10
Large	6
Medium	4
Small	3

Management
- Finalisation of cleaning, security, furniture, flowers, telephone and service hire contracts. Schedule chasing.
- Liaison with client re PR, publicity, press releases and supply of press pictures. Press day tickets and invitations. Reception organisation, uniforms for stand staff. Control of artistic fits and tantrums.

Client
- Selection and appointment of stand staff as above.

Design
- Final visits, quality checks and control. Dimension checks, visits to all workshops and inspection of near-finished models, effects and A/V.
- Control of artistic fits and tantrums. Briefing of site supervising staff, depending on size and type of project.
- Clearance of diary for on-site run up to completion.

	PHASE 7
CATEGORY	WEEKS
Major	6
Large	2
Medium	2
Small	1

Management

On Site
50 per cent of time

- Keeping the client/curatorial staff away. Panic control.
- Final typing of all loose ends. Organisation of reception.
- Details of VIP visits, security, toilets etc. Resolving of site wrangles re delivery, permissions, missing orders, missing exhibits.

Client

- Staying away; thinking about the next project. Anywhere but on site.

Design

On Site
50 per cent of time

- Close attention to construction – is it the right way round? Right site? Right exhibition?
- Supervision of installation of special effects, models, objects, exhibits. Graphic designer supervising packing and delivery of graphic panels.
- Low profile supervision of *all* site work and any extras agreed on site. Resisting emotional blackmail.

	PHASE 8
CATEGORY	WEEKS
Major	0
Large	0
Medium	0
Small	0

Management

Opening and/or press day
- Passing all credit on to supervisors.
- Looking humble.
- Walking backwards.
- Dabbing away designer's tears of pride or shame.
- Keeping a sharp eye on special effects, working exhibits and the drinks cupboard.

Client

- Smiling as if he had done it all himself.

Design

- Trying not to look pleased with self. Passing all credit a little too obviously. Walking backwards, sulking, crying. Keeping a sharp eye on all working exhibits.
- Going off to drink with production team and contractors, and anyone who will listen.

	PHASE 9
CATEGORY	WEEKS
Major	0–0.5
Large	0–0.5
Medium	0–0.5
Small	0–0.5

Management	• Record photographs. Post mortem. • Final account settling and agreement (bills to be paid on receipt).
Client	• Post mortem.
Design	• Post mortem. Explaining overspends. • Thanking ALL involved for extra efforts etc.

The preceding chart will of course have holes in it, and is necessarily full of generalisations, but it should serve as a guide to aspiring managers and hopefully as a stimulus to designers, to appreciate the need for good management. In truth, no matter how creative the design team, and how sophisticated the client, management can make or break any project.

Good management, like good design, is not conspicuous and the modesty and maturity needed to fulfil this behind-the-scenes but vital role are difficult to develop. All design needs management, and the sooner this is recognised by all design colleges and architectural schools, the better. At the moment, good managers are born and not made. If the designer on any project has to concentrate on all the aspects of production detailed in the previous pages, the creative input and attention to detail will suffer, to the detriment of the finished product.

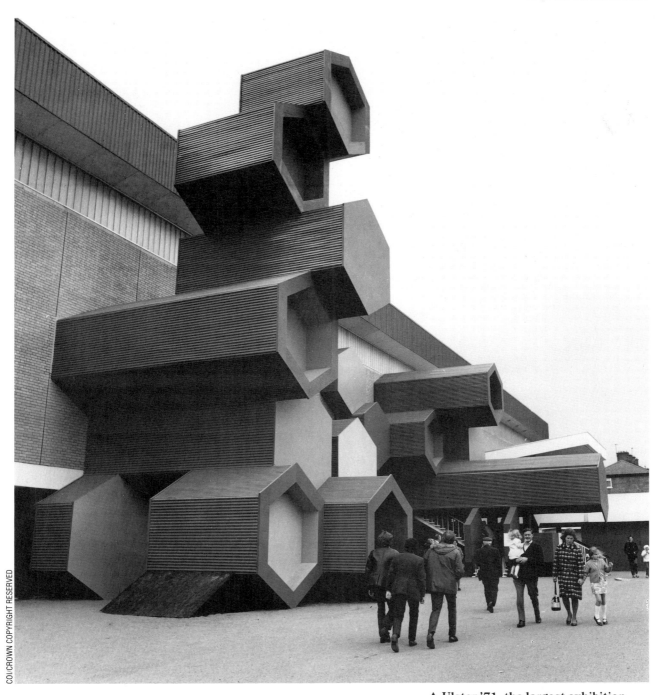

▲ Ulster '71, the largest exhibition of its type since the Festival of Britain. It was produced in eighteen months by a team consisting of a project leader-cum-scriptwriter, two managers, two 3D designers and a graphic designer. The erection was supervised on site in Belfast by an installation officer.

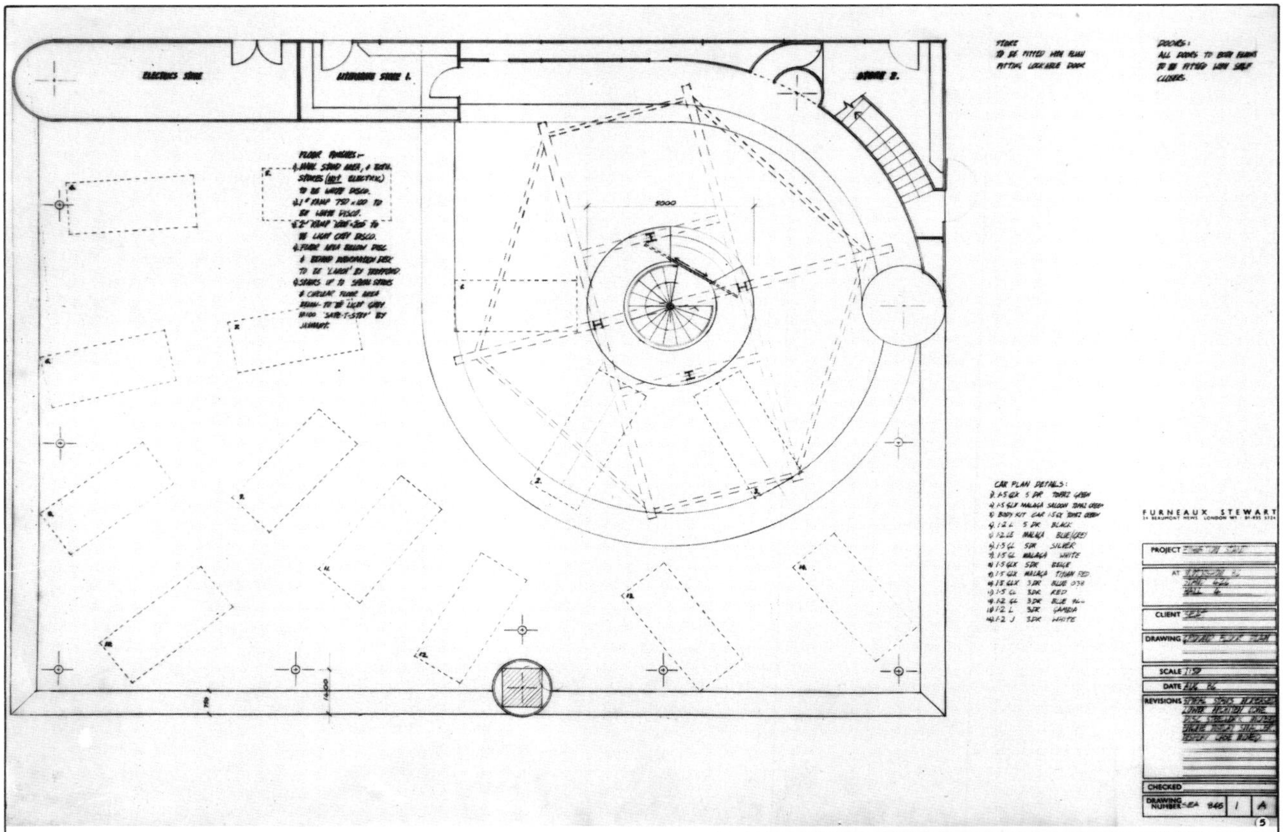

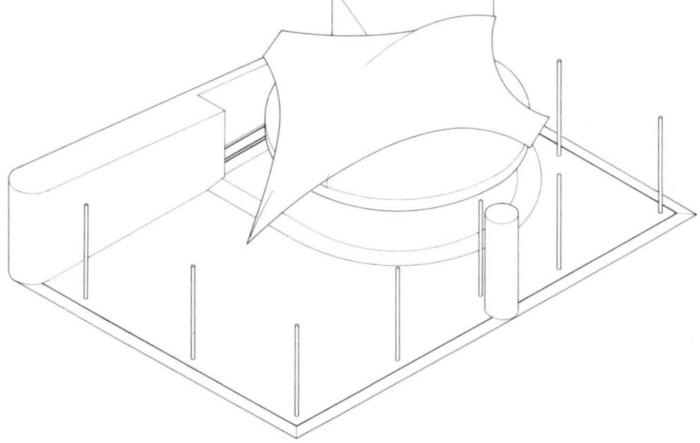

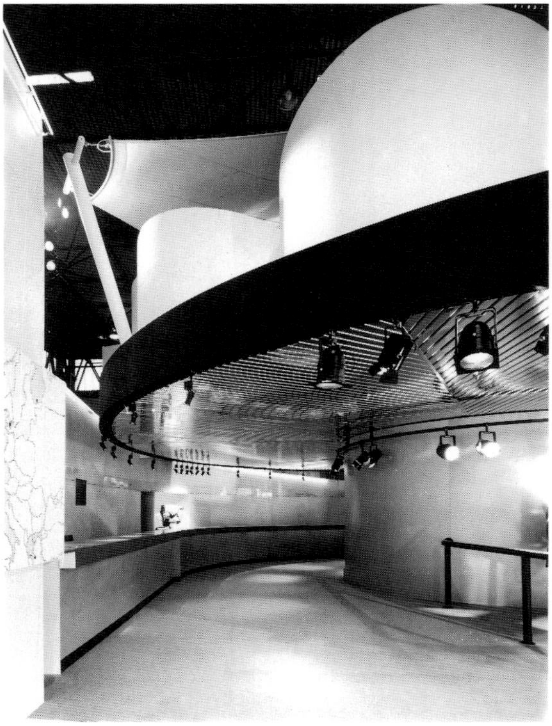

FURNEAUX STEWART AND SEAT CONCESSIONAIRES UK LTD/NICHOLAS GENTILLI

7

THE PRODUCTION

After all the creative work, the assembling of the information and the objects, and after the discussions involved — the ideas, proposals and rejected schemes — comes the practical side; the actual production of the exhibition. For some people this is the most exciting part of the process; for others it is simply a procedural necessity after the stimulating early stages. In any event it is essential and, while many of these processes are devolved from the design and management into the hands of specialists, the previous chapter showed that constant supervision is required throughout. This supervision is not because the specialists are inadequate or inexperienced, but because the communication of complex and often original ideas from the designer to the maker is a difficult and sometimes unsatisfactory process. Here face-to-face explanations, briefing and ongoing consultation is frequently the best method.

DESIGN PRESENTATION

The primary means of communicating the design to manufacturers is by drawings. There are two types: accurate 'scale' drawings and visuals or perspectives, sometimes called 'artist's impressions' which show what the finished product should look like. The visuals are useful, to give an idea of the appearance of the end product, but the scale drawings are essential. A scale drawing is an accurate plan with elevations (side views) and sections (cuts through) drawn neatly in ink or pencil on to tracing paper. Scale in this context means that on the drawings, one centimetre might represent one metre. This is shown as 1:100, or an inch might represent one foot, shown as 1″ to 1′0″. There are many variations on these scales, but clearly all drawings should either be done in the metric or duodecimal system. A small scale metric drawing to show whole plans and elevation will be 1:100 and a small scale duodecimal drawing will be ⅛″ to 1′0″. For normal purposes, section details of construction, showcases, handrails, stairs etc might be drawn to a large scale at 1:5 metric or 3″ to 1′0″ (ie quarter full size) duodecimal.

The design is drawn on to tracing paper for two reasons; first so that an accumulation of previously worked-out detail sketches can be traced off, and second so that the several copies needed can be printed by a process known as dye-line printing. This process uses light passing through the tracing paper and not through the drawn line to print the line drawn on to plain paper. The multiplicity of copies is required for estimating,

◄ A plan containing specification details, top and right. The best place for company name, scale etc is bottom right.

◄◄ A visual of the same exhibition stand.

◄ The finished article: Furneaux Stewart's prize-winning stand for SEAT cars at the 1986 Motor Show.

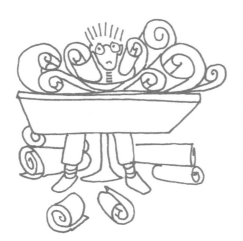

sub-contracting and construction stages. Dye-line printing is cheap and commonplace, and more or less true to scale. Since all papers shrink and expand slightly, depending on humidity and climate, important dimensions should always be written on to drawings as well as being drawn as accurately as possible.

A good working drawing is orderly, well laid out and explicit. It should be read at best from left to right and from top to bottom. If the plan, sections and elevations are on one sheet, then the plan should be at the bottom, with elevations over it and sections to the right. The plan should have the sides from where the elevations are 'viewed' clearly marked, along with the 'cut' lines of the sections. All the text on the drawings should be written clearly in a good hand, or applied in stencilled lettering. Wherever possible, this lettering should be horizontal; sometimes however dimensions are shown running along the line, so a height would involve vertical writing — always pointing in the same direction. The best drawings contain all the relevant information including the code numbers of other drawings upon which large-scale details can be found. It is worth remembering that these drawings are read by many different people, so the name of the design organisation, together with project designer, draughtsperson and appropriate telephone numbers should be on the drawing, preferably placed in a box set in the bottom right hand corner of the drawing, where it can easily be found. Drawings should never be rolled, and always folded. Rolled drawings can become unmanageable and the user will become enmeshed in a quire of rolls from which he may never emerge. The correct way to fold a drawing is so that it lies flat for the user when unfolded and reveals the design firm's name when folded up.

The first destination of the working drawing is the contractor's office. Exhibition contractors exist as specialist organisations. If they cannot be traced locally, then shopfitting firms undertake the same work. Firms are often specialists in both. Sometimes the 'small works' division of a building contractor will undertake exhibition work. Both permanent and temporary exhibitions are specialist work. A great deal of quick thinking is required from all involved, from the contractor's representative, through the workshop manager, the estimator and the craftspeople — carpenters, painters and signwriters on the shop floor. The latter are in fact a special breed, often despised by their more conventional fellows because they are always willing to attempt anything, to cut corners, to solve problems in a way that is not at all 'by the book' in order to achieve some special finish or detail. The mixture of woodworking and display demands a certain delicacy of touch, a sensitivity, a lateral thinker who is constrained neither by training, nor by set solutions. The same is true of all craftspeople in the field, frequently being asked to take either personal or professional risks to solve the problems that arise. The very fact of deadlines adds to the instant nature of the work; the show must open on time. Occasionally, even after the most careful planning, 'ghosters' (all night work) have to be done to complete on time and, despite the difficulty, the camaraderie developed under circumstances like this is often rewarding and memorable. At best it is a very stimulating business where management, designers and craftspeople are equal in their efforts to obtain the best results.

The Estimator

The person who brings together any contractor with any designer is essentially the estimator, for it is the competitive price that wins the contract. The estimator is a specialist who goes over the drawings millimetre by millimetre, costing out everything to be used in the construction. To this end a certain amount of written information will be helpful. This can be either, as has been said, on the drawing or separately, in the form of a specification. The former method has the advantage that all the information is to hand for both the estimator and the maker, but it is quite common and satisfactory for a separate, detailed specification to be typed up, to be read in conjunction with the drawings. The estimator will literally price every nail, screw or piece of wallpaper to be used in the construction which, along with an estimation of the time it will take to build and transport; of subsistence, contingencies and profit, will constitute the price the contractor submits to his potential client. Most estimating is done in competition with other contractors to the client's price advantage, but it is only possible to compete fairly when identical drawings, specifications and estimating time are given to each competitor.

When estimates are required from individual specialists, artists or modelmakers, it is impossible to go in for competitive tendering. The input from each craftsperson will be different and the briefing will differ from one individual to another, depending upon the ideas thrown up at the time. It is a good idea under these circumstances to select a craftsperson who will best respond to a particular problem and either ask for an estimate of the cost of the agreed solution, or to allocate a certain sum within which to work. This is of course an area where experience and knowledge of a wide range of specialists is invaluable. No matter what, both sorts of contractor need good working drawings. They serve to define clearly the space within which the specialist is to work. The second major use of working drawings is actually to construct the exhibition. The drawings go first to the works manager, who will be briefed by the estimator and if possible the designer, to ensure no misunderstandings and to effect any changes that the estimator might have recommended. The job supervisor, usually an experienced craftsperson, will also suggest changes and short cuts, and these must be discussed. From the manager and supervisor, the drawings will go to a setter out. This is a draughtsperson who will draw up everything to full size on huge sheets of paper. These are sometimes called 'rods' after lengths of wood marked up to show accurate running dimensions for use in workshops or building sites. These rods are used by

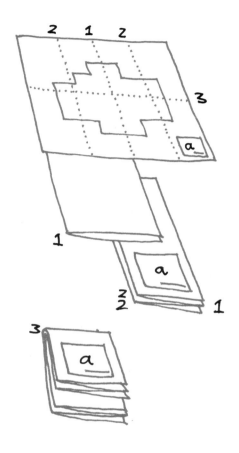

▲ The correct way to fold a drawing
fold 1 onto itself, in half
fold 2 each half back to expose
       drawing title 'a'
fold 3 in half lengthwise, title 'a' still
       exposed

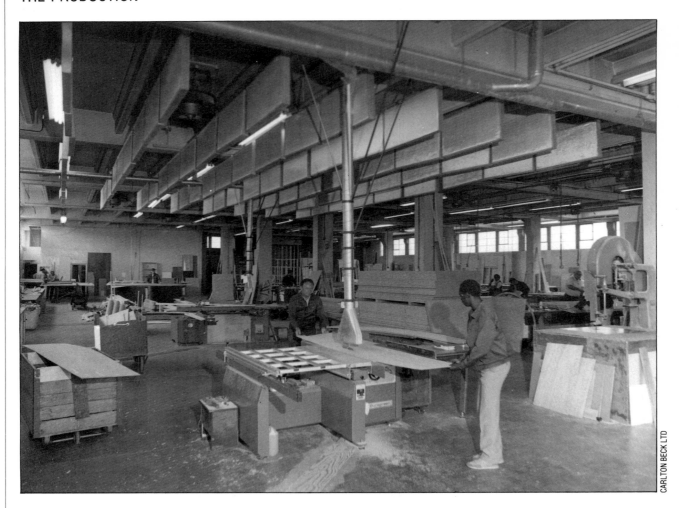

CARLTON BECK LTD

▲ **A typical exhibition contractor's workshop. Carlton Beck Ltd, London.**

the carpenters who can measure off at full size the work they have to do. In many contractors' premises there are cutting workshops, where all the timbers or boards are cut to size and then delivered to the joiners. A big job will be given a supervisor at this stage and a team of carpenters, who will generally stay with the job from the shop floor to the exhibition site. A good designer will take an interest at all these stages and get to know the supervisor and the team. Good relationships and a respect for the craftspeople's skills will lead far more surely to a good finished product than absentee dictation of requirements. The contractor's workshop, if you are encouraged to visit (and you only will be if you behave properly in it) is fascinating.

Systems

Another method of construction entails the use of systems. These are prefabricated units which can be bought or hired and assembled in a number of different ways. Many systems come with a miniature kit which can be used to assist the design process. The amount of creativity and true design work involved when using a system is clearly less than when starting from scratch, but it is not to be scorned unless it is misused; for example, either specified by a non-designer to avoid using a designer, or used by a designer as a lazy solution to a problem. Their main use is for shell schemes or for exhibition stands which need to be erected and dismantled several times. They are also abused when they are considered simply as vehicles for graphic displays with no consideration given to planning or circulation. There are of course systems which are better than others, which naturally cannot be quoted here, but the best of them offer the widest possible versatility for the least amount of expenditure. The best systems are also recessive in character and do not proclaim their origins; exhibitions are, after all, for selling goods other than systems. The oldest system is the stock panel, generally $2400 \times 1200 \times 50$ mm ply on batten, used over and over again for shell schemes, or straightforward exhibition walls.

Contractors

Not only do the carpenters turn flat drawings into three-dimensional structures, but the electricians are doing early off-site wiring of light boxes etc, and the painters are undercoating or spray finishing special units. The artwork shop is preparing full size layouts for cut-out lettering and finally, if double-deckers or metal structures are involved, the metal work is taking shape in the metal shop. A contractor's workshop is no place for the clumsy, the insensitive or the garrulous, so visits should be carefully planned and arranged to be of maximum value to the progress of the job and the least inconvenient to the contractor. The same is true of visits to the specialist craftsperson. Every moment of time is money within the tight profit margins of small companies; posses of grey-suited designers, managers and clients taking up space in the middle of a workshop are not welcome unless strictly needed.

Sub-contractors Some exhibition contractors sub-contract certain bits of work. This is entirely up to them, though there are a limited number of specialist sub-contractors. In time, most designers get to know those in their area quite well. The main tasks to be sub-contracted are electrical and metal work, photographic enlargements, screen printing and sometimes painting and decorating.

The main contractor will often have a regular association with the sub-contractors and will simply ask them for a price, but occasionally will go out to tender. To this end, further copies of the drawings may be requested, specifically marked up or highlighted for perhaps electrical work or decorative finishes. This marking up is done in one of two ways. The first method is by having a second tracing copied, using the dye-line process. New details can then be added to this and more ordinary dye-lines made. The second method, on perhaps a less complex job, is to see an ordinary dye-line of the original tracing and mark on to it with coloured felt pens the extra information. In either of these ways, electrical, decorative or special effects mark ups can be produced for distribution. Obviously, the latter type cannot be reproduced, and are generally made only after a contract has been let to clarify work for the single successful contractor.

The sub-contractors will be supervised by the main contractor, and requests for changes or expressions of concern about their work should always go through the main contractor — partly out of simple politeness, but also to avoid confusion.

Specialist contractors Special-effects contractors are generally supervised by the designers and, when there is one, the supplier of the technical information that the special effect is intended to communicate. It is essential that they should supervise together, the designer because of the interpretative and constructional elements, and the specialist to ensure that the effect accurately represents the science, technology or historical facts involved.

Away from major cities, it is frequently difficult to find special-effects makers. The author is frequently asked where to find such people. It should never be impossible. Modelmaking, for instance, is a more or less common profession; the *Yellow Pages* or their equivalent will have a section for them, but enquiries among architects or surveyors should elicit some names of modelmakers. They often have, or can quickly acquire, other skills such as diorama making. Some are good at exact representations from architects' or engineers' drawings; others show

▼ **A flight simulator: inside, apparent reality . . .**

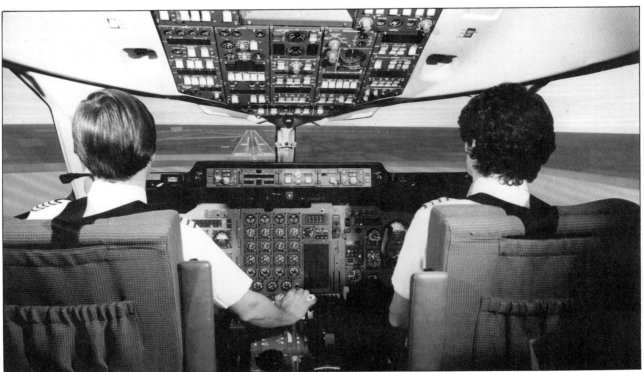

REDIFFUSION SIMULATION LTD

strengths with figures, animals or vegetation. Taxidermists can also be found through the *Yellow Pages*, local natural history societies or museums.

There are craftspeople who specialise in plastics or metals. There are carpenters who specialise in pattern making. These can often be tracked down through suppliers of basic materials. Visits to modelmaking or hobby shops can prove profitable, as the shopkeepers are invariably knowledgeable and helpful, and often experts themselves in one field or another. There are craftspeople who specialise in cut-away models or artefacts, or cut-away drawings. Most car manufacturers or consumer durable manufacturers need prototypes, instruction leaflets or training manuals and photographs for publicity and generally will be delighted to pass on names, particularly if their company name will appear with a grateful acknowledgement in the credits for the exhibition. Sculptors and artists, unless very well established, are generally willing to take on commissioned work. If models of people or animals are needed, or murals or backdrops, then approaches to local arts societies can often prove profitable. Again, the *Yellow Pages* under 'artists' agents' could be useful.

Some of the finest landscape models are made for flight simulators in the aircraft industry and are frequently associated with considerable electronic ingenuity. Aircraft companies or airlines should be able to provide information on the specialists they use. Some of the most sophisticated, yet commonplace, electronics is found in the world of microcomputers and TV, video and sound

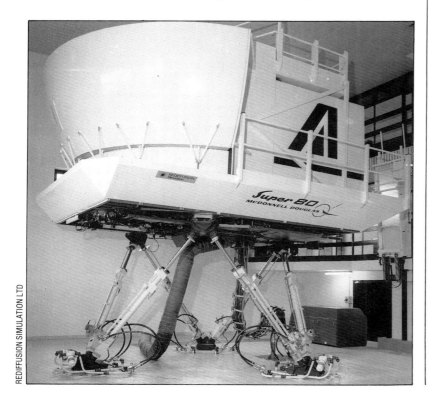

REDIFFUSION SIMULATION LTD

◄ . . . outside, the truth.

All of the expertise and technology used to produce these very expensive simulators can also be used on a much smaller scale for special effects in exhibtions.

reproduction and cameras; again, shopkeepers themselves may know of specialists. Pursuing lines of enquiry, starting at the simplest level, can prove rewarding and interesting. If computer drawing or graphics is required then, at the time of writing, this is really only found in large metropolitan areas, but the sophistication of these devices rises in direct proportion to the rate at which the costs — and therefore availability — drop. Today's magic is tomorrow's standard equipment, and the space between today and tomorrow is shrinking all the time. Advertising agencies are another good source of information on models or animators; often one sees a commercial containing a technique or style exactly suited to solving a particular problem. But, be careful — animated film and indeed all purpose-made film is an expensive solution to a communication problem. Graphic designers and illustrators can be traced through advertisers or publishing companies. Keep a lookout for styles or gimmicks that are suitable for certain solutions and always make a note of anything that might be useful one day, and track it down there and then.

Always look at the work of any specialist with an eye to the possible application of it, or the materials involved, to your

▼ **A drawing done by a computer.**

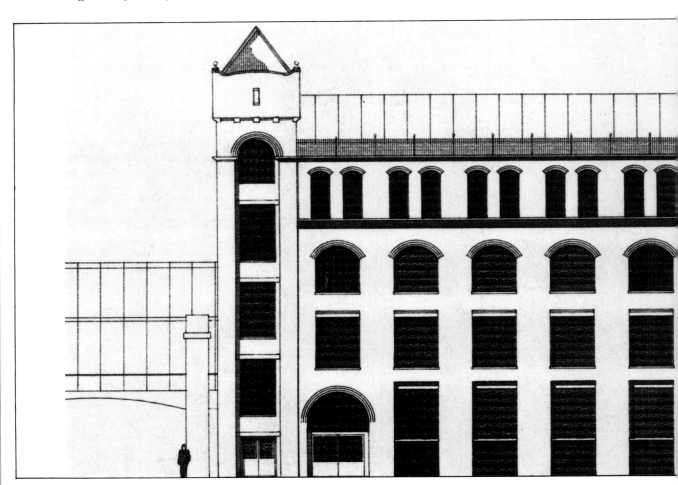

needs. The dentist makes accurate, fast, moulded reproductions. Out of what? Where do the blacksmith, the watchmaker, the imaginative car mechanic exist? Who makes that button or machine, the engraved plate on that engine, that back-lit instruction panel, that video game in a motorway café? No matter what, special-effects makers are made and not born. They evolve through accidental meetings and bizarre requests into geniuses who can make anything from a space ship for a film to a fossil tree texture in GRP to clad an exhibition showcase.

SITE CONSTRUCTION

Once all the parts of an exhibition that can be made in a workshop have been completed, then — dates permitting — work on site can commence. In a commercial exhibition this is generally a matter of days, but even in an exhibition in a special venue or a museum, work away from the workshop always costs more; therefore site work is best kept to a minimum. The first thing to get right in a commercial venue is the orientation of the stand. On island sites this can prove to be a problem; they have been known to be built the wrong way round. The designer should check, if

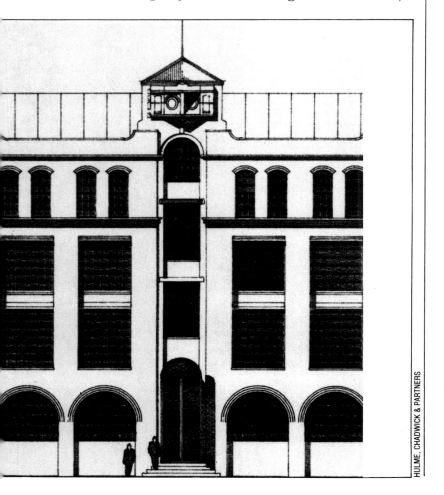

HULME, CHADWICK & PARTNERS

there is a shadow of doubt, by visiting the site on the first morning of the build-up. Once checked, then any electrical conduiting can be laid in or services tapped before the platform is built (usually 100 mm high). Most major structures have platforms; lesser shell scheme stands or booths rarely do. The platform generally consists of 80 mm × 50 mm unplaned timbers on edge with a 20 mm board covering. On top of this flat finish, a carpet or special floor finish is laid early on and then protected with heavy duty polythene stapled over it until opening day. Cutting carpet or PVC around complex exhibits is time-consuming and eventually wasteful; as a quantity of exhibition carpet is re-used, it is best to build the exhibition over it. This does not apply in museums, where it is rare to have a platform. Usually a carpet or special finish is laid directly on to the floor. This generally means that all services have to be brought in at high level, which is an important consideration at the design stage. It should also be remembered that for permanent structures in public buildings, there are sets of safety standards somewhat different from those permitted for a short time on an exhibition site. When specifying for such work, it should be made clear on drawings and specifications that such local or national rules should be respected by main and sub-contractors. Some design organisations have a special stamp made to this effect, for use on all drawings. This ensures that the responsibility lies with the contractor and, in the event of default, the blame will be correctly apportioned, since the designer cannot possibly check in detail all the joints made, materials used and fireproofing activities undertaken.

If the exhibition is a trade fair booth or stall, then the walls and a rudimentary floor covering will have been provided. For a professional-looking job, the floor covering should be jettisoned, or the organisers should have been asked to omit it. It is possible to put up a professional-looking stand within a shell scheme, and it is generally worth it, but only if a completely new structure is erected within it. The organisers' permission must be obtained and their rules adhered to, but it is still possible, and the end result will stand out from its surroundings: the main aim!

If metal work is required for a double-decker structure, this is often the first part to be put down; sometimes before the platform unless the load needs to be spread and the entire area beneath the board covering to the platform spread with stout timbers, upon which the steel work can be placed and bolted. Once the platform is in place and carpeted, and the metal work complete, the carpenters can be let loose to construct the exhibition. At this stage, site visits become important but they should be discreet and short. Work should not be delayed in those deadline circumstances by either chat or an absent designer who is needed to explain confusing drawings or changes in detailing. There are specialist site supervisors, clerks of works or installation officers employed by large organisations for large or complex exhibitions. They are comprehensively briefed by design and management, and maintain a constant but low profile on site, discreetly checking all details, answering questions and commissioning in writing extras that are absolutely necessary. On-site extras are a costly business, first because site time is expensive and second, with a designer's mistake, rectification is absolutely necessary, so it will not be cheap. The answer is not to make mistakes. If the contractor makes a mistake, he will pay for it.

Once the bulk of the joinery work is done, the painters will arrive. However, normally in the organised rush, painters, carpenters and electricians will work around each other with the painter doing essential tidying up after holes have been made for the electrician. They should all be attended by a labourer or two on site to clean up continually, as accidents happen in messy circumstances. People working to meet a deadline can trip over flexes covered by wood shavings perhaps, and serious injuries may ensue.

There is a peculiar feature about contractors working on temporary exhibitions: everything is hired. This means in fact that every part of the exhibition, although made to the designer's specifications, remains the property of the builder. Peculiar shapes or cases are generally scrapped at the end of the show, but stock wall panels can be retained, as can platforms, carpets, fascia boards, beams or metal work. Some of it goes for scrap, but electrical fittings are always kept; lamps, tubes, plug sockets and tops can all be re-used. This hire procedure actually reduces costs for the client and probably started in order to ensure that the contractor turned up at the end of the show to clear away the exhibit. Obviously, it does not apply to permanent work or, indeed, if the client wishes to buy a special feature, arrangements can be made with the contractor.

Hiring applies elsewhere. All standard furniture can be selected from catalogues of firms accredited by the organisers; to buy items for short periods is clearly absurd. There are firms specialising in the hire of plants and flowers and their attendant accessories. The firm will also maintain the plants during the course of the exhibition.

At the appropriate time the exhibits, special effects, models and so on are delivered to the site. The designer or site officer should supervise their unloading and delivery to the stand, their unpacking and their installation. If there are valuable exhibits, this is the time that security guards arrive. With valuable and/or fragile exhibits, the specialists should be the people to unpack them and to attend to their installation and display. As can be imagined, by now the site is buzzing with activity: craftspersons of all kinds, special-effects people, specialists, security officers and design and management. If possible, the client must be kept away. Unless he is very experienced and relaxed he will almost certainly be in a state of panic, concerned that the show will not open on time: 'How can all this mess be cleared up by tomorrow?' 'Where is this one to be displayed?' The best place for him is in his own office, available in case of disaster or essential change.

It is, however, an expensive time for change. Design, as has been shown, involves thinking something through as a whole enterprise, planning it carefully, drawing it accurately and supervising it closely through workshops and studios. To feel constrained to change things on site is a sign, first that this process has not been as thorough as it should have been and second, that the designer (and this is serious) is not capable of the careful forethought necessary. Assuming he or she is thorough and capable, then a desire to change is simply a demonstration of insecurity and lack of confidence, and should be resisted, for it will inevitably be a mistake. In fact, the exhibition will never look right until it is complete; since it was conceived as a whole, it must emerge as a whole before being assessed. Then, absolutely essential fine adjustments can be made.

In all these circumstances, the client is best elsewhere. He is neither trained nor experienced in visualising, and is likely to turn up on site, notice innumerable unfinished details and then hare around telling everybody — who already know — what needs fixing, painting or illustrating. It is to be hoped that no actual or potential 'client' will be offended, reading this: he is not being accused of incompetence.

Just as the client is a fish out of water before the exhibition is complete, so the designer is completely spare once the exhibition is open.

8

THE COMPLETION

The ideal time for the client to arrive on site, even if he has sneaked the odd look from a distance beforehand, is just as the cleaners are stripping off the protective coverings from the displays. The sheets of polythene are cleared away from the carpet and wrapped exhibits; the designer is making final adjustments to the lighting; a single painter is wandering around with a small brush and a paint pot or two, searching for missed patches or scratches to be covered. The manager is standing, rubbing his hands and rocking back on tired feet and calf muscles, and the installation officer — if there is one — is amiably arguing with the contractor's representative over sheaves of notes about extras. That is a good time to arrive.

The stand is emerging like a butterfly from a chrysalis and is, hopefully, a little ahead of its neighbours; certainly better, bigger and in a more favourable position. The press are expected in a few minutes and suddenly there is the client, a trolley full of drinks and glasses behind him. A posse of attractive company representatives, fresh and interested, are moving through the staff areas checking space, orientation and facilities of one sort or another; while brochures and sales literature are being loaded onto counters and leaflet racks.

THE CLIENT

At this point, there is only one thing the designer needs from the client: solid, undiluted, hyperbolic praise. No matter what criticisms there are (and they will emerge soon enough), at this moment emotions are running high and even the most objective criticism will be taken as a personal insult.

If the client is seriously unhappy, then he and the manager must get together to try and resolve the situation. Errors arising at this stage must be the result of poor communications, in which case the client and the design team are both at fault. The client's wishes have been wilfully ignored by the designer; or the client's delegate has not communicated adequately with his seniors. The solution to poor communication between designer and client is compromise; the solution to wilful designer behaviour, sometimes called artistic temperament, is for the designer to be lured away from the site completely while the management sorts it out. This is, however, very bad practice and should not happen. The solution to poor communication in the client organisation is for the senior client to buy his way out of the problem, provided that there is time.

In a well-ordered world, none of these calamities should come to pass. However, nobody can avoid certain problems — for example, non-deliveries because of weather or natural disasters, small slip-ups when working abroad, unavailability of a certain tool or connector, a missing crate. Nevertheless, these should have been foreseen or spotted early on by the site supervisor, so should not present problems immediately prior to the opening of the exhibition.

THE PRESS

If there is a press preview, it is often unofficially permissible (though most exhibition rules forbid it in writing) for work to be completed while the press are around. It is forbidden because there are two sets of rules in public exhibition halls; one for when only the stand constructors and exhibitors are there and another for when the press and public arrive. One of the most important of the rules applies to clear gangways for escape in case of fire, so if the work is continuing it can sometimes be got away with if it is low-profile and the gangway is kept clear of packaging or waiting exhibits. It is common practice, however, for many finishing touches to be applied at the feet of the journalists who turn up on press day.

Finally, the exhibition — be it trade fair stand or museum, gallery or heritage centre — is finished in every way. Exhibition staff are ready, in uniform or neatly dressed. The cleaners have clattered away, flicking off the last bits of dust as they left and everything is gleaming like a new pin. Everybody involved has had a good look round, checked every exhibit and read every label for misprints. The graphic designer has gone over every panel or label, touching out white specks with black and black with white, meticulously tidying where even the most sharp-eyed visitor will never look. The designer, smartly dressed and inwardly nervous, is outwardly calm and talks with one eye on a colleague and the other on the approach of a VIP or senior client.

THE PUBLIC

Then the public arrive. They take everything for granted, swooping and picking, homing in on the areas the designer hates and ignoring areas of gigantic effort. The only place for the designer now is to be relaxing at home, with a big drink and a sympathetic ear for the tribulations of the past weeks; a comforting presence as the exhausted genius worries darkly about whether the whole concoction will last the days, weeks, months or years for which it has been created.

ASSESSMENT

Sadly, this is not the end of the matter, for the best time to assess the successes or failures during production is quite soon after the opening. The job is fresh in the mind, the mistakes are clear and have not been rationalised out of existence, and the good aspects are immediately evident. A post mortem is not just

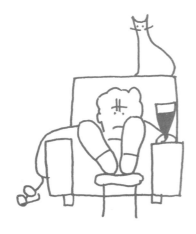

the evaluation of the exhibition's qualities; it is the evaluation of production. With the client safely tucked up with the new acquisition, it is a good time to take stock and highlight areas of misunderstanding and failures in scheduling or delivery, or to discuss strengths and weaknesses in the production team. The best place for the post mortem is in a café on site, for the other important aspect is the immediate observation of visitor reaction, both to the specific exhibition stand and, almost equally importantly, the competition. A calm walk around an exhibition or trade fair with the colleagues involved in the production can be very rewarding. Objectivity is hard to come by after days of single-minded involvement, but an attempt at objective appraisal of the exhibition or stand and comparison of solutions will be invaluable. Most trade fairs have a theme; therefore many designers will have been trying to solve similar problems of display, communication and construction. It will be well worth assessing these other solutions, for something can be learned from everything.

This kind of assessment is in fact the secret portfolio of a good designer. Sheer experience is an unbeatable commodity, and though the final chapter dwells on scientific attempts at objective appraisal, there is nothing so valuable to the designer as personal experience and observation.

While the on-site post mortem is of great value, it will be far too early to assess the real results of any particular enterprise. In a permanent exhibition, the early post mortem will take place on or near the site, and the reasons for it are the same as for the temporary exhibition. The real long-term assessment of the value of certain treatments and design approaches will emerge, when it is considered cost effective, from professional assessment of the results of the exhibition described in the final chapter.

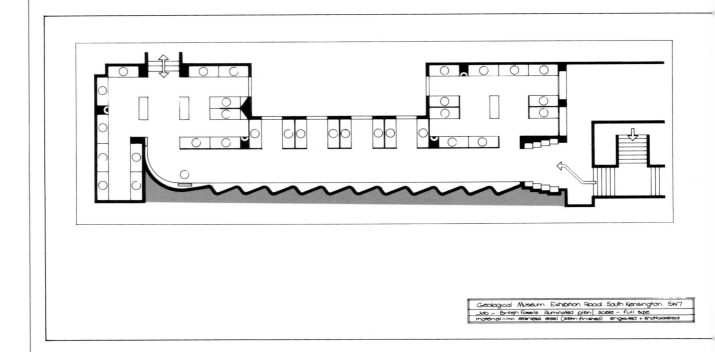

Geological Museum. Exhibition Road. South Kensington. SW7
Job ~ British Fossils illuminated plan scale ~ full size
material ~ 1mm stainless steel (satin finished) engraved + shotblasted

9
THE MAINTENANCE

T here is one solid fact about exhibitions; no technically sophisticated enterprise should be embarked upon without the certain knowledge that it can be maintained. There is an old maxim which says that there is nothing worse than a working exhibit that doesn't work. There are many worse things, actually, but old professionals like their old saws. Basically, do not start something which cannot be finished. This applies to anything that might be expected to fail or give trouble during a period of three days or more, and this of course includes lamps. Even the most simple illuminated display should be left with a small stock of replacement lamps when it is handed over to the client. If they are not all used, they would almost certainly have been needed if they were not there. This circumstance obviously ranges from simple lamp changing to the replacement of working parts in a sophisticated piece of technical equipment.

ACCESS

The primary consideration is of course access. This can be gained to a display from nearly every direction, but it must be built in. The best possible access, space provided, is from the rear. In a museum exhibition it is wise to allow a maintenance passage or alleyway all round the perimeter of the site. Thus, if the exhibition is introverted, within a room or hall, then a passageway at least 600 mm wide, accessible preferably from outside the exhibition, should be provided. This is naturally only a guide; introverted exhibitions come in many forms. If showcases are back to back and there is no front access, often avoided for security reasons, then a spur to the access passage might run up between them both for maintenance and for dressing. If access has to be provided from the front, then a secure, preferably invisible method of locking must be used. There are many, but certainly avoid anything with an exposed 'keyhole'. Little fingers (and sometimes big ones) stuff little things into keyholes. For some reason this is an irresistible temptation, the worst of which is chewing gum.

Top access can be given but it is frequently difficult, as with front access, to carry out essential maintenance during the open hours of the exhibition or museum. All these points apply equally to temporary exhibitions or stands; access must be considered, planned and built in. The best way to get it absolutely right is to consult with the technicians who will have to carry out the maintenance. Not only can they advise on access, but also on

◄ **A maintenance alley. 'British Fossils', Geological Museum, 1980.**

153

types of equipment which give less trouble than others. Some light fittings become infamous for the speed with which they consume lamps. All sorts of projectors have lamps, some better than others, some with automatic lamp-changing facilities. On really sophisticated set ups, a unified maintenance facility is built in. In the US Pavilion at the Knoxville World Fair in Tennessee in 1982, a central control room not only contained all the video players required throughout the pavilion, but also monitored the failure of electronic devices in the building. The Air and Space Museum in Washington has the same facility. Both of these were new, purpose-built structures in which it is comparatively easy to build such services. At Disney World and Epcot, Florida, all the displays, restaurants and events are linked by an underground network of passages so that the whole campus can be serviced discreetly. In national museums in the UK and France, for instance, interference with the structure is frequently restricted by the inhibitions imposed by the 'listed' architecture, but there is no reason why — with attentive planning — good service facilities cannot be built in, in consultation with technicians and engineers.

SERVICING AND EQUIPMENT

Temporary exhibitions are frequently serviced by the contractors or companies renting out the equipment. Flowers, for instance, which are by no means a technical exhibit but thought by some to enhance an exhibition stand, are hired out and maintained by their owners. The same is true of projection equipment, but if there are purpose-made special effects then ease of maintenance must be part of the brief in the first place and special arrangements must be made.

Water is generally considered a nightmare on any exhibition stand; not as a facility (normal plumbing can cope with that), but either as a decorative feature or part of a technical exhibit. Pools and fountains can give a great deal of trouble if the plastic waterproofing is pierced accidentally (or deliberately), or the pump fails. Water should only be used when it is essential to the display. If it is completely enclosed, then condensation will prove a problem unless forced ventilation is introduced. On a long-term exhibit, fungicides should be used in distilled water to avoid discoloration. Outdoors, water is far less trouble.

When considering A/V presentations, there are one or two factors that need attention. For permanent displays, slides need replacing regularly, particularly if it is a non-stop display. It is best to have the display activated by the arrival of visitors, and this can be done either with pressure-pad switches beneath the carpeting, or ultrasonic or radar devices which sense the arrival of the visitor. If projection is the only way the pictures can be shown because of a large screen size or the demands of the physical circumstances, then stay with projection, but if circumstances permit, television monitors are worth thinking about with video tapes or discs. The latter are virtually indestructible; the former will wear out but not nearly as rapidly as film. Again, these can be automatically activated but at the time of writing, cost for cost and considering maintenance problems there are advantages to both methods, depending on permanence and physical circumstances. The same is true of sound reproduction. Again, at the time of writing solid state sound is just coming on to the market, and clearly prices will drop and recording time lengths will extend; it presents a real solution to the problem of maintaining players and the quality of sound reproduction.

When *buying* all types of equipment, the availability of spares must be considered. Brand new developments might be exciting, but when they rapidly out-date or are superseded, then spares become a problem. For a temporary exhibition, if a technical device is purchased then spares should be bought as part of the package, so that there will be no nasty surprises. It is rather like the good sense of taking vital car spares when motoring abroad.

There are some electronic or mechanical devices that are more stable and reliable than others; for instance, with slow revolves it is always wise to purchase a model that will bear a far heavier weight than actually required.

Running tungsten lamps at a lower voltage than that for which they are designed makes for a greatly lengthened life, but this is not possible with low voltage or fluorescent tubes. A TV set needs less maintenance and is far more reliable than a sophisticated projector. There are also techniques which are more durable than others and therefore demand less attention. Ciba prints and slides last far longer than ordinary ones. Black and white photographs are virtually indestructible, except by vandalism. Actual artwork should never be used for graphic panels, always a photograph of it. Then, if it fades or is damaged, a new print can be made from the original negative. The same applies to typographic displays: never use the actual typesetting, always a print. Ultraviolet is the great enemy of colour. Filters can be applied to windows if direct sunlight is anywhere near to displays.

SECURITY AND SURVEILLANCE

Security can present a problem for maintenance if there are valuable exhibits which also need proximate attention to equipment. Security guards have to be on hand while cases are opened and fittings changed. This is not because any of the maintenance crew are unreliable or dishonest, but because it is unfair to load the responsibility of security on to them. They are neither trained nor paid for it. Security or surveillance is the only real answer to vandalism which is rare in the countryside and provincial museums, but certainly common in national museums in the UK. It takes the form either of mindless assault — spraying sweet sticky substances such as Coca Cola, which is hard to remove, or bunging up holes with chewing gum or sweet papers; or concerted vandalism when indelible felt-tip markers are deliberately taken into museums to damage artwork and fabric. Not only is vandalism more prevalent in inner-city areas, but it applies also, it seems, to boring or incomprehensible exhibits. This is in its own ghastly way understandable, if one thinks in terms of kicking in the television set (an inclination quite innocent people have had at one time or another).

OPERATING CONDITIONS

Another aspect of maintenance applies to equipment used to make life in an exhibition more bearable. This applies to fans, air conditioning and dust proofing. Again, it is a burden if not maintained adequately. Air conditioning needs regular maintenance, and when showcases or areas of sensitive equipment are dust-proofed, the filters have to be changed regularly or the whole system becomes useless. This refers to showcases in which the exhibits are kept clean by pumping filtered air into them at a high enough pressure to keep the dirty air out. Obviously this is much more necessary in an urban atmosphere than in the cool, cleaner countryside. Again, this type of equipment, when used for short-term exhibitions, can be hired, so the maintenance can be hired along with it, daily checks being made by the contractor who has the franchise for that particular exhibition.

When changes of staff are necessitated for temporary or permanent exhibitions, it is important that the new staff should be fully briefed with regard to maintenance. To this end it is useful to have maintenance schedules and documents which are regularly updated for every contingency.

The final aspect of maintenance is simple cleaning. For temporary exhibitions at trade fairs, cleaning contractors exist and are generally franchised. They should attend daily before opening time to vacuum all floors, collect rubbish and dust showcases and exposed exhibits. This is standard practice, and when exhibition organisers publish their rules of attendance, such contractors are listed. In 'one-off' special exhibits, clearly special arrangements should be made.

Museums and galleries generally have either their own cleaning staff, or contract cleaning staff to do the work. These again should be attended by security staff when necessary, but specialist cleaning staff should be employed where particular attention is necessary. The days of dusty, obscure museums ought to be over, now that such an interest in the past is taken by the public.

Maintenance therefore is a job for professionals. They need to be consulted early, considered throughout and employed specifically. Whether they are contract or salaried, they are vital to the continued success of any exhibition. For portable or mobile exhibitions, employment must be considered at each venue, or the travelling display will suffer. Any final assessment of the success or failure of any exhibition must take into account its maintainability and the planning of any exhibition must learn from the successes or failures of previous ventures in this respect, as in any other.

10
THE RESULTS

Evaluation has become something of a catch word in exhibition design, particularly in the design of large museum exhibitions. In North America there are even government agencies charged with the responsibility of evaluating large public programmes to establish whether taxpayers' money has been well spent. It is not surprising that in these circumstances evaluation can be seen as a rather threatening activity. A team of evaluators forms a jury and a government official, acting as judge, passes sentence. But the defendant — usually the designer — is not given the chance of representing himself.

This aspect of evaluation requires fuller consideration, in particular how such destructive and potentially recriminatory situations can be avoided. Before doing so, however, a few words about the meaning of evaluation might be useful.

Put very simply, evaluation is an activity that seeks to discover the extent to which something — in this case an exhibition — has succeeded in achieving its purpose. There is also a more constructive focus for evaluation and this is to make recommendations about how an exhibition might be improved to achieve its aims more effectively.

This description of evaluation does, however, beg a rather important question, namely, what was it that the exhibition set out to achieve in the first place? The brief should contain all the data to be communicated, but if an exhibition has been mounted without a clearly defined purpose then any evaluation of it would be rather pointless. For example, in evaluating a computer exhibition, if it were found that the exhibition failed to communicate to 50 per cent of the OAP visitors the difference between RAM and ROM, the exhibition's designer could always claim that this was never one of his purposes in designing the exhibition.

Having said this, setting objectives for an exhibition is not easy; and setting standards which, if met, would indicate that an exhibition had been successful is even more of a problem. Success is rather a slippery concept. A workmanlike approach is to define the target audience for whom the exhibition has been designed. In the case of a commercial exhibition the audiences could be users of the products on display, the trade, or the company's own sales staff. An exhibition might be designed to achieve different things for these different audiences. A company might want to convince the consumer that its products were superior to those of its competitors in some very specific respects. It might want to ensure that its dealers reached the hospitality suite, if nothing else; and it might want its own sales staff to feel proud of the company.

Once the audiences have been defined, the design team can begin by writing down what it hopes each of these audiences will take with them from the exhibition. Space precludes a full discussion of the art of writing objectives, although much can be achieved by defining what each of the audiences is expected to *think*, *feel* and *do* having seen an exhibition, that it did not think, feel or do beforehand. Once the audiences have been defined and the exhibition's aims stated, the evaluator can consider ways of finding out the extent to which the aims have been successful for each of the audiences. The ways in which an evaluator goes about doing this will be considered in due course.

One of the objections sometimes raised against the formal system of evaluation is that it is largely superfluous to the process of design. It is argued that the designer is constantly evaluating his own work to see if he can find ways of improving it. The designer, according to the argument, by virtue of his professional training, is in the best position to evaluate design solutions. For example, a designer constantly reviews floor plans in the light of his observations and the expected flow of visitors and he experiments with different typographic styles so that the right emphasis is given in the right place at the right time. Experience tells him when things are right, when things are likely to work or not. Perhaps an evaluator without this experience is likely to simplify and make matters trivial by failing to visualise the design of an exhibition as a complex and integrated whole. Perhaps an exhibition is more than the sum of the parts an evaluator might study. An evaluator who puts parts of an exhibition under the microscope may fail to see how they relate to the grand plan; and any recommendation to change parts of an exhibition could even have an overall detrimental effect. After all, there is no logical reason why an improvement in one small aspect of an exhibition might not diminish some other part of it. A good exhibition is all about balance, and for one part of it to be successful might suggest that another part will be less successful.

A second, closely related argument is the view held by some designers that design is a wholly intuitive and creative activity; and any investigation into this process is in itself likely to subvert the very ends that good design hopes to achieve. This is, in fact, a modern exposition of a very ancient view in which creativity was thought of as a kind of divine madness, a seizure of the individual by the gods. As usual, the Greeks had a word for it: *enthousiasmos* which means 'God, within'. An awareness of this view may partly explain the rejection by some designers of any evaluation or research into the effectiveness of exhibitions.

There are a number of things to be said about these arguments. First, any evaluator who fails to acknowledge the professional skills of the designer, not least the designer's ability to evaluate his own work, is unlikely to produce anything that is worthwhile or anything that will be taken seriously. What the professional evaluator has to offer, over and above the evaluative skills of the designer, is a training that allows him to take a more dispassionate, objective look at how an exhibition is likely to function or has functioned among the audiences for whom it was intended. This training allows the evaluator to move beyond subjective opinion about what visitors will or will not, did or did not, get out of an exhibition, and to talk objectively, with some degree of precision and authority about visitors and their reactions to an exhibition. His skills are similar to those of a market researcher or an account planner in an advertising agency. If there is any doubt whether these skills are thought to be useful, it is worth noting that today it is almost inconceivable for a new product or advertising campaign to be launched without detailed consumer reactions being provided by market researchers and account planners throughout all stages of development from early concepts to the final products or commercials. The reason why this sort of information is often lacking in exhibition development may have more to do with a lack of accountability than a lack of usefulness. Businesses depend on the success of their products or services for their survival, whereas many museums and art galleries, certainly the publicly funded ones, are less concerned with direct financial returns.

Of course, this argument about lack of accountability should not apply to commercial exhibitions, and yet formal evaluations of commercial exhibitions are rare indeed. One of the reasons for this state of affairs is that exhibition budgets can be small in comparison with other elements in a company's total advertising and marketing budgets. Exhibitions also tend to be thought of as being less critical than other marketing activities in stimulating sales. But times are changing. The number of large, industry-based exhibitions has increased dramatically in the past few years and the costs of exhibiting have likewise increased significantly. The costs of mounting transient displays in major exhibitions can be enormous and, therefore, before long, companies will begin to ask questions about the effectiveness of their exhibitions to see whether their money is being wisely spent.

So much for the arguments in favour of objective evaluation; but what about those so-called objective evaluations that fail to understand the nature of design, that fail to see the process and products of design in their entirety? It has to be said that no matter how sophisticated the techniques used by the professional evaluator, there is always the possibility of error and misjudgement; and the evaluator's techniques can never be guaranteed to give worthwhile results if they are used by evaluators who are insensitive to designers and the design process. If an evaluator lacks this sensitivity there is no guarantee that he will direct his techniques at the things that will really matter. The uninformed will sometimes be able to spot wrong answers but it takes a creative and sensitive mind to spot wrong questions, or situations where questions might be the wrong method and observation more appropriate.

One of the ways of nurturing and encouraging this sensitivity is to place evaluation within the context of a team approach to exhibition design, with designers and evaluators working alongside each other. Thinking of the evaluator as the person who comes along after all the work has been done and the exhibition has been opened is a prescription for insensitive, irrelevant and not particularly useful evaluation. Indeed, the most successful and useful work provided by evaluation is usually when an evaluator has been employed during *all* stages of the design process.

Finally, before turning to the kinds of information that an evaluator might most usefully provide, a few words are needed concerning the relationship between evaluation and the intuitive view of design. The most important comment to be made in this context is that exhibition evaluations are not concerned with delving into designers' innermost workings but with providing information and guidelines that will help designers to produce more effective exhibitions for their intended audiences. The evaluator's focus of attention, and the designer's, must be the visitors, and developing an understanding of how visitors perceive and relate to the information and objects on display. As such, evaluation complements the design process and should not be set in opposition to it. In the final analysis successful exhibitions will always depend to a large extent on the creative leaps of the imagination that the designer can make with, among other things, the information provided by an evaluator. The evaluator is there simply to help the designer know more about the topography of those leaps.

TYPES OF EVALUATION

In the previous section it was mentioned that the most successful evaluations are those where the evaluator has been employed as a member of the design team throughout the design process. In the early stages, before the designer makes any marks on paper, the evaluator can assist in preparing the brief. During the design stage, the evaluator can assist in evaluating several courses of action by 'testing' each of them in mock-up form; and, of course, once an exhibition has been opened, the evaluator can be concerned with trying to find out how successful or effective it was.

Experience suggests that the most useful types of evaluation are those that take place before an exhibition is built. The reasons for this are twofold. First, at the beginning of a project, the people involved in it are more open-minded and less committed to any particular course of action so evaluation data provided at this stage has more chance of being noticed and acted upon than information that crops up when a project is well under way. This is particularly true if the information provided by the evaluator is critical of what has been done, or if it questions decisions that have already been taken. Second, if things are shown to be wrong *after* a decision has been taken, the majority of people involved in the decision-making process may be concerned primarily with establishing that what went wrong was not their fault.

It does not take much imagination to realise that in these circumstances the evaluator is not going to be the most popular person, and that his comments are likely to seem threatening to the people whose activities have come under his scrutiny.

────────────────── Concept Research ──────────────────

Once the client has decided that an exhibition is to be mounted, the task is to evaluate the various ways of approaching the subject and to define, as clearly as possible, the target audiences for the exhibition. If published data is available, assumptions about the nature of the audiences can be compared with the actual facts that are known about them. If it is not possible to get a clear picture of the audiences from the available information, the evaluator should recommend commissioning a sample survey in which their characteristics can be measured at an acceptable level of precision. These characteristics should include such demographic statistics as age, gender, and socio-economic class, but additional information about the background knowledge and interests of the target audiences for the exhibition should be collected to give the design team the clearest possible picture.

Exhibitions set out to communicate to visitors in various ways. At the pre-planning stage, the evaluator will help to formalise the various messages as unambiguously as possible. Despite doubts that may be raised about the use of objectives they are critical if the design team is to keep a tight rein on its aims and intended achievements. During the early stages of development, however, objectives should not be thought of as immutable; indeed, they are almost bound to change as the process of development unfolds and as the design team becomes more familiar with the topics and what can be achieved in the exhibition. Nevertheless, they should always form the yardstick for evaluating progress.

At this stage, the evaluator will also be concerned with the conceptual framework and the strategy around which the information in the exhibition is to be structured. There are many different ways of threading together a set of ideas to come up with the same underlying message or messages. It is important to adopt a strategy that fully exploits the appeal of the exhibition to the target audience. If the design team does not have a sound basis upon which to make a decision between the various options, the evaluator may recommend commissioning visitor research to help in defining the strategic approach to be adopted in the exhibition. The form of this research is often termed concept research. Essentially, this involves presenting the various options to a representative sample of the target audience in story form and inviting their reactions. At this point, the evaluator will be looking at the pros and cons of the different options.

────────────────── Creative Development ──────────────────

Whereas evaluation at the concept stage is rather speculative since it deals with plans that nobody has as yet tried to imple-

161

ment, evaluation at the creative development stage focuses on things that are actually happening.

Formative evaluation

As soon as the designer makes an attempt to implement the agreed strategy, steps can be taken to evaluate the success with which the implementation is proceeding. These evaluations are aimed at shaping the form of the final product.

The evaluator will usually carry out research on 'mock-up' displays to check whether they are achieving the desired reactions from visitors. Feedback will thus be gained on how the displays are working and what effect they are having.

Consumer reactions have to be interpreted with considerable sensitivity to stimulate the creative process further and to ensure that good ideas are not killed simply because they were not properly presented in mock-up form.

Evaluations using mock-ups are usually conducted among small samples representative of the target audience in an open-ended and qualitative fashion since the main emphasis is on discovering how the content might be better represented. The strength of an effective rational argument is more likely to be apparent despite crude presentation since arguments depend on logically and psychologically constructed prose rather than typography and graphics. It is clear that evaluations of a mock-up will not indicate a great deal about the emotional appeal of a display as it would appear in a real exhibition.

The outcome of these early evaluations will typically take the form of discussions between the evaluator and the designer in which proposals for remedying any weak points in the communications will be put forward.

Objective evaluation

Before an exhibition is built it may be necessary to obtain approval from the client.

Often the designer will have produced a three-dimensional model or visual of the exhibition, together with a detailed specification of the products/artefacts to be included as well as the accompanying text and graphics. It is at this stage that final approval for the designs is sought and the evaluator's role is to produce the objective evidence that has been collected which justifies the proposed design solutions. The evaluator will help provide reassurances on how and why the particular exhibition will work among its intended audience.

Summative evaluation

After the exhibition has opened, the evaluator will be concerned with discovering the impact of the exhibition upon its visitors. Among other things, he will be interested in establishing the extent to which the objectives or aims of the exhibition have been met and whether the exhibition can be improved upon in any way and if so, how. This will not apply to short-term exhibitions.

Perhaps the major purpose in evaluating an exhibition after it is opened to the public is that it provides the evaluator, and through him the design team, with the opportunity of learning from their mistakes. The information thus collected should be assimilated by the design team so that they can avoid making similar mistakes in the future.

──────── THE PSYCHOLOGY OF EVALUATION ────────

Before concluding this chapter, it is worth considering what is likely to happen when an evaluator has presented his findings, and how his evaluations are likely to be received. Much of what has been written about the uses of the data provided by systematic evaluations seems to rest on the assumption that the data will be seen as information about the ways in which the exhibition has performed against certain expected standards of success. In other words, evaluation data is seen as providing information about possible improvements to exhibits. Behind this assumption lie at least two more related assumptions, neither of which is necessarily warranted. One is that the kind of data provided by the professional evaluator is clear-cut and open to only one sort of interpretation. The other is that everyone will want to act in accordance with the recommendations put forward by the evaluator on the basis of his findings. Let us consider each of these assumptions in turn.

Shortly after the publication of *The Origin of Species* in 1859, Engels wrote to Marx, commending Darwin's book and claiming that in it was a natural justification of Marx's theories. In marked contrast, political pundits of a different bent interpreted Darwin's theory as a natural justification for unfettered competition in the social sphere. George Bernard Shaw described these attempts in the Preface to *Back to Methuselah* as follows:

> 'Never in history as far as we know, had there been such a determined, richly subsidised, politically organised attempt to persuade the human race that all progress, all prosperity, all salvation, individual and social, depend on the unrestrained conflict for food and money, on the suppression and elimination of the weak by the strong, on Free Trade, Free Contract, Free Competition, Natural Liberty, Laissez-faire: in short, on "doing the other fellow down" with impunity.'

Apart from observing that times have not changed a great deal the interesting question, psychologically, is how can different people interpret the same facts in diametrically opposite ways?

When a person evaluates something he does so in the light of the beliefs he holds. If the thing he evaluates conforms to his own view of the world, he evaluates it favourably. If it does not, he either rejects it as being of no value or he construes it so that it *does* conform. The important point to note is that an individual very rarely adjusts his own beliefs in the light of 'the facts'. (This is hardly surprising since a person with a constantly changing set of beliefs would soon begin to feel he was losing his grip on life.) So, contrary to popular belief, facts rarely, if ever, speak for themselves. Facts are invariably interpreted before any conclusions are reached; indeed, if facts speak at all, their voices originate within us.

All of this places the evaluator under some considerable difficulty. Whereas he might reasonably expect people to agree with the facts he has collected through a process of systematic study, he cannot reasonably expect everybody to agree with his interpretation of them and, accordingly, he should not expect people to accept his recommendations as a matter of course. One way the evaluator can avoid this predicament is to draw up a number of scenarios as to the possible outcomes of any evaluation study *before* actually carrying out the study. These scenarios should include conditional courses of action. Having done this, the next task is get all the people concerned to agree to these courses of action; again, this needs to be done before the study is carried out. As the reader might imagine, all this is a lot easier said than done since most people like to keep their options open, particularly if they feel threatened in any way.

Notwithstanding the problems the evaluator might have in getting other people to agree with his interpretations, what of the situation where nobody disagrees with them, or at least not publicly? Can he, in these circumstances, expect the force of his arguments to prevail, and for the recommended courses of action to be followed? Unfortunately, the answer is 'no' since it is always possible for people simply to ignore uncomfortable facts. If an institution is not held accountable in any meaningful sense then no amount of objective evidence will necessarily affect the way it acts.

Perhaps the observations in this section have convinced the reader of the opposite argument to that intended, namely that professional evaluation is no more likely to help designers produce effective exhibitions than any other kind of evaluation. Nevertheless, it is hoped that there is a clear and intelligent case to be made for professional evaluation; and providing there is a will to act upon such findings, the practical benefits should be apparent.

GLOSSARY

Acrylic A thermoplastic of the same type as Perspex or Plexiglass, usually transparent.

Air and Space The name for various museums, particularly the one in Washington DC, part of the Smithsonian.

Aisle The space between lines of exhibition stands. The central or main passage between exhibits.

Approval The stage at which a client's final agreement to a design scheme is given.

Animation The art of making animated cartoon films. Hence the term 'animated film' for a serious production.

Animated model A model of a person or animal which moves, simulating reality.

Ambient light The actual, overall light level of an exhibition environment.

Artefacts Old or new man-made objects.

Artist's impression A drawing done by a designer to give an impression of how an exhibition (or building) will look on completion.

Artwork The original material done by an illustrator or graphic designer for reproducing on to display panels.

A/V Audio-visual. An effect using both sound and vision; generally slide shows.

Backdrop A flat painted, coloured or photographed screen or scene behind a display to give an illusion of place or space.

Back-lit Lit from the back, particularly a transparent photograph.

Back-projection Projected from behind the viewing screen, which is translucent.

Bold A heavy, big-bodied typeface.

Books on legs A derogatory name for any display or exhibition with too many words.

Booth A small stall or partially enclosed shell scheme stand at a trade fair.

Brief A concise synopsis of the requirements.

Budget The actual financial allocation to any particular project.

Buried loop A transmitting circuit built in to an exhibition to carry an audio commentary.

By laws Local regulations which control structures, aisle widths and opening hours of exhibitions and particularly fire precautions.

Clerk of Works (Usually to do with the building trade.) A specialist supervisor of all site work.

Commentary The recorded, spoken accompaniment to a display, A/V programme or sequence of special effects.

Commercial attaché The member of an embassy staff in charge of trade or business affairs.

Commissions Contractual arrangements with specialist craftspeople or sub-contractors.

Concept research The backing up of ideas with study as to practicability and effectiveness.

Conceptual framework A specified notion of the form in which ideas are to be expressed.

Condensed A narrow, close-packed typeface.

Conduiting Tubing or ducting, in metal or plastic, usually used to carry electrical services.

Conferences Large business or professional gatherings, in this context usually associated with exhibitions.

Conservation The science of preserving our heritage; hence conservator: a specialist in a field of conservation.

Context The subject range of an exhibition.

Contract The legally binding arrangement as to cost and time between a contractor and the client.

Copywriter One who writes text for exhibitions or programmes.

Cornice A decorative detail or moulding between walls and ceiling to effect a neat joint or give an impression of greater height or width.

Counter As in a shop, used by receptionists or stand staff to dispense literature etc.

Craftsperson A skilled, trained maker of things; a carpenter, painter or modeller.

Creative development The examination and expansion of subject matter to produce presentation ideas.

Credit An acknowledgement of a person's or company's contribution to a production, usually on a Credit Panel in a prominent part of an exhibition.

Critical path The line emerging from a production schedule, showing the relative time by which all tasks must be complete.

Cross-fade To change a projected still picture by fading down from one and up on the other, using two projectors on to the same screen.

Curator A person in charge of a museum or objects in a museum. Usually the source of information for a museum exhibition.

Cut-away A man-made object with a piece removed neatly to expose its workings.

Cut-away diagram A drawing to explain any object representing part of the object removed to expose the inside.

Cut-out lettering Lettering made by cutting out sheet material to the shape of letters or logos.

Detail A small, intimate piece of design, drawn at full size; hence detail drawing.

Diorama A three-dimensional display, part-model, part-painting. A working diorama: one with moving or lighting parts to simulate activity.

Disc A video disc containing pictorial information as stills, or moving images with a sound track.

Double-decker An exhibition stand or construction composed of two decks or floors.

Double-sided A display panel, case or area that can be seen from each side.

Draft Any non-final version of scripts, storyboards or treatments.

Draughtsperson A specialist in drawing up designs.

Drawing board A smooth, flat board on which drawings are prepared, usually with accurate horizontal and vertical line drawing instruments.

Dressing The art of displaying objects in a showcase attractively and effectively.

Duodecimal The system of measurement using twelve parts to a measure, ie 12″ to 1′0″. A foot is technically obsolete in the UK but is still commonly used. It remains in use in the USA.

Dust-proof A sealed case or showcase. A case into which filtered air is pushed faster than unfiltered air can drift in.

Dye-line A method of reproducing drawings done on tracing paper.

Ecocentre A public place devoted to exhibitions of local ecology and its interpretation. It is most common in France.

Edge lighting The effect caused by light travelling laterally across Perspex sheeting and being emitted at the edge or where the sheet is engraved, using clear, coloured or fluorescent Perspex.

Electronics The technology of the use of electrical systems for special effects and display devices.

Elevation A drawing done to scale of the side view of an exhibition.

Entertainment space Private or secluded space set aside for the entertainment of important visitors; hospitality suite.

Estimate The carefully calculated cost of a piece of construction; often produced in competition with other contractors.

Evaluation The science of assessing the worth or usefulness of something. Testing an exhibition's possibilities of success beforehand. Assessing reaction during, and summarising the results afterwards.

Exhibition A fair, show, display, expo or any display of objects for select or public view.

Exhibition contractor Company or individual specialising in building exhibitions.

Exhibition space Part of an exhibition set aside for display.

Exhibitor A company or company's representative initiating or taking part in an exhibition.

External lighting Light coming from outside an exhibition.

Extra Any item not included in the original drawings or estimates and therefore executed on site.

Extrovert exhibition One designed to be approached or appreciated from the outside, on an island or near-island site.

Eye level The height of the eye relative to the display. For general purposes, approximately 1600 mm above floor level for adults. Special allowances should be made for children.

Fade To lower lighting levels. See cross-fade.

Fair An exhibition, display or show of goods and objects for commercial reasons. A fun fair.

Fascia board The board at the front or leading edges of an exhibition to carry titles, names etc.

Fibre optics Flexible glass or plastic fibres which carry light for great distances. Either optically correct or for illumination only.

Film loop A continuous loop of film giving repeated showings of the same sequence.

Fire resistant Will not immediately catch fire, but will eventually.

Flat display Text and pictures only.

Flight simulator A complex device to train pilots using a mock-up cockpit and models and videos of airports, landscapes and flight situations.

Fluorescent Substances which glow when an electric current is passed through them, or a powerful light is shone on them.

Franchise A special arrangement whereby a contractor, or a selected group of contractors, can supply services to a trade fair or major exhibition.

Front silvered mirror Glass silvered on its face to give a very true reflection, due to the absence of a thickness of glass between the image and the viewer.

Fungicide A chemical used to kill fungi which might otherwise colour or spoil water displays.

Gallery An art gallery. A part of a major museum. A raised walkway.

Gangway The aisle or space between exhibits at a trade fair.

Geodesic dome A light, strong structure made by combining a grid of triangular elements formed from rods and fabrics.

Geological reserve A large area of outstanding geological interest, usually with interpretative exhibitions at the centre or sites of special interest.

Ghost An image produced by projection on gauze or screen material.

Ghoster All night work on an exhibition; 'doing a ghoster'.

Glass painting Paintings on the back of one or more layers of glass or clear Perspex giving at best a deep, luminescent image.

Graphics Flat two-dimensional treatment of images and text.

GRP Glass reinforced plastic. A plastic or resin made and formed cold, and reinforced with glass fibres.

Halogen An element which, alone or in conjunction with quartz, produces a hot powerful light when electricity is passed through it.

Handrail A safety rail on a staircase or balcony, or a rail to keep the public at a distance from the exhibits.

Handset As on a telephone. A method of communicating a commentary without disturbing other visitors.

Headroom Space beneath overhead structure to allow for easy movement and circulation.

Heritage centre A place for the exhibition and interpretation of the local built environment.

Hologram An image made photographically, with laser light, to give an impression of three dimensions.

Imex A film and projection system using 70 mm film stock and special sound effects to create a powerful impression of real movement on a massive, close screen.

Indemnity A type of insurance or guarantee made by the government to cover the cost of loss or damage.

Industrial shed A prefabricated structure made for factory use.

Inflatable Any structure made with inflatable bars joined by fabric or a structure with sealed doors kept up by constant pressure.

Informative display Simply to inform.

Infra red Invisible light used to activate proximity switches etc.

Installation officer A specialist who supervises all the construction work on an exhibition site.

Italic A sloping typeface.

Interactive A type of display which responds to the visitor's input.

Interpreting The word used to describe the activity of designers and writers simplifying complex information produced by specialists, for easy comprehension by ordinary people.

Introvert exhibition One designed to be appreciated entirely from within, in an enclosed space.

Island site An exhibition site with no immediate neighbours; isolated by aisles or gangways.

Keyboard A matrix of buttons with numbers, letters or symbols giving access to a computer-controlled display.

Laser A narrow, intense and accurate beam of light used to make holograms or dramatic lighting effects.

Label The short text and its 'card' directly concerning an exhibit. Its title, size, provenance, code number etc.

Layout A plan showing the positions of parts of the story, exhibits and displays.

Light A slim, delicately wrought typeface.

Light-box A white or silvered box with an opal top and fluorescent lights used to back-light photographs, transparencies or slides.

Linear lighting Lighting along a line or set of lines, or behind a cornice or skirting, to give effects of distance, division or space.

Literature Reading material freely available in an exhibition.

Loop absorber A box of spools used to contain, in a compact form, a loop of cine film.

Maintenance The support required for electrical or special effects of one kind or another. See Chapter 9.

Management A vital part of the production process: its organisation. See Chapter 6.

Massing The positioning of solid or semi-solid objects relative to each other.

Mechanical engineering The technology required for the design and manufacture of special effects and display devices of one sort or another.

Medium A typeface between light and bold in weight.

Mock-up A full-size model of a display, clearly temporary, used for evaluating a display's potential or workability.

Model An accurate small scale representation in three dimensions.

Moiré A watery pattern from watered silk or mohair. A pattern arising from one set of lines passing in front of another.

Multi-screen An audio-visual presentation of slides or TV on more than one screen.

Multi-decker An exhibition stand on two or more floors.

Mural A large painting, photograph or photomontage. A representational wall covering.

Narrative The story or theme of an exhibition.

Negative The transparent, reversed film image from which a print is made.

Neon A gas which glows red when charged with an electric current. Gives its name to various gases in bent glass tubes giving off bright coloured light.

One-off A single purpose-made exhibit or device.

Opal Semi-translucent white glass or plastic used between the source of light and a transparency.

Organiser The official sponsor and co-ordinator of a commercial exhibition.

Panel The name for part of a wall in an exhibition, normally of light construction and non-load bearing, 2.4 x 1.2 x 0.05m. A display panel: one carrying graphic material.

Partition The normal name for an exhibition wall made up from stock panels as above.

Pavilion A special, generally temporary building erected to contain a national exhibition at a world or trade fair.

Penalty clause A term in a contract, imposing an agreed fine on late delivery.

Pepper's Ghost A device for replacing one three-dimensional image gradually with another in the same place.

Perspective A drawing done by a designer to give an impression of how an exhibition will look on completion.

Perspex A form of thermoplastic of extreme clarity used in place of glass.

Plastic laminate Opaque, hard, durable, variously coloured and textured surface finishes.

Platform A wooden plinth, usually 100mm high, upon which large commercial exhibition stands are built.

Polaroid© Light polarising material used for animated diagrams.

Portfolio The book or folder of photographs of work by a designer or design firm.

Post mortem An examination of the problems that arose during production.

Pre-planning The stage before the actual planning when ideas are being evaluated and discussed.

Presentation A word sometimes used to describe a display. The showing of a scheme to a client.

Press day The day immediately before an exhibition opens, set aside for visiting journalists.

Press release A special piece of literature with pictures for distribution to the press.

Pressure pad A switch set beneath a carpet to activate a display on the visitor's arrival.

Production chart A diagram produced by hand or computer to define production stages or phases.

Production schedule The listed deadline dates for all phases of production.

Program The specific set of instructions and responses inserted into a computer.

Programme A timed sequence of sounds and/or pictures to convey a story or message.

Projector A device for projecting a sharp, focused image, either still or moving.

Project manager The manager appointed for one particular project.

Proof reading The meticulous reading and correcting of all text or copy for a project to spot factual, spelling or typographical errors.

Public space Areas allocated for the use or passage of the public.

Pulsed tape A tape emitting signals to initiate activities or effects.

Purpose made Made for that exact purpose only, one-off.

Quartz A silicon mineral which, in conjunction with other elements and electricity, produces a bright light.

Radar Radio signals, the interruption of which can activate a switch.

Radio Short wave or buried loop. A means of communicating within an exhibition to individual visitors in specific areas.

Random access Swift access to pictures and/or text via projectors or disc players, facilitated by a computer.

Recessive A style of design or presentation wherein the objects on display totally dominate the design treatment.

Record photographs Photographs taken immediately on completion of an exhibition to record its pristine appearance. Vital for portfolios.

Replica An apparently exact reproduction of anything from a jewel to a steam engine.

Representative (Rep) Generally a sales person present on a commercial exhibition stand and essential to its function.

Reproduction The general name for the many methods of copying pictures and text for display purposes.

Revolves Continuous or pulsed turntables of any size.

Rods A term sometimes used for 'setting out' drawings.

Rotagraphics® A patented device for changing a picture or sign three times within the same flat plane. See Toblerone.

Rotosign© A patented device for producing many back- or front-lit pictures within the same flat area.

Section A drawing showing what an exhibition, display or detail might look like if cut straight through. An explanatory drawing.

Semi-silvered glass Literally glass half-obscured by silvering, used for making Pepper's Ghosts.

Set square A triangular instrument with one right angle used for resting on a T square to produce accurate drawings.

Setting out Producing drawings at full size from scale drawings for the use of craftspeople.

Scale The comparative measurements used for drawings and translating.

Scenario A skeleton of a dramatic work or a whole exhibition.

Science centre A museum or exhibition centre devoted to explaining science by example and interaction.

Screens White or silvered solid or translucent surfaces to receive projection. Divisions between one area and another.

Screen printing A method of printing using photographically produced stencils.

Script writer A specialist in producing researched text for an exhibition or commentary.

Shell scheme A lay-out of booths or stalls for a trade fair providing walls, fascias, lighting and minimal floor covering.

Showcase A glazed, secure box for displaying objects.

Shopfitter A company specialising in building shop fronts and interiors, and sometimes exhibitions.

Simplified keyboard A limited number of buttons giving access to a computer-controlled display.

Site The actual geographical location of an exhibition or its position within a trade fair.

Site supervisor A specialist who supervises all the construction work on the exhibition site.

Skirting A space between walls and floor protected by being recessed or covered in durable material.

Solid state Computers, sound or pictures contained in a device with no moving parts.

Specification A document describing exactly the work to be done.

Special effects Any electronic, mechanical (or both) device for communicating or enhancing a display.

Split screen One screen on to which are projected several different but associated images.

Stall A small booth or enclosure at a trade fair or market.

Stand The usual name for an exhibition construction at a trade fair or special exhibition.

Stencil A method of printing where ink or paint is pushed through an outline to leave a precise shape.

Storyboard A set of drawings with associated text in rough book form which acts as the specification for an animated film or slide programme.

Story line The main gist or theme of an exhibition or programme.

Stripping off The removal of all protective coverings from an exhibition immediately prior to opening.

Synopsis A brief, concise description of the requirements of an exhibition.

System A prefabricated exhibition construction kit.

Systematic A manner of displaying information in an ordered way, using relative factors found within the subject.

T square A largely obsolete, T-shaped drawing instrument, the cross bar of which rides up and down the edge of a drawing board, making the stem of the T a perfect horizontal. See set square.

Tableaux Life-size presentations using models, artefacts and clothes to re-create a possible scene of bygone years or contemporary life.

'Talking Head'© A talking face projected on to a white relief model which, with a sound track, gives the illusion of a real person talking.

Taxonomy Classification, or classification principles.

Technomation© A patented system which uses Polaroid© to simulate movement in back-lit diagrams.

Tender An estimate document, usually competitive; another word for estimate.

Thematic A way of ordering an exhibition based on a narrative.

Thermoplastic A plastic made and formed using heat.

Tier A level in a hierarchic display. A seating level.

Tilt A tilting mechanism.

Toblerone® A Swiss chocolate bar, equilaterally triangular in section, giving its name to any part of a display device that resembles it. See Rotagraphics®.

Trade fair An exhibition, display or show of goods or objects for commercial exposition.

Transparency A transparent photograph which has to be viewed on or with a light-box.

Treatment A concise description of the method of presenting information using illustrations, objects and text.

TTS True to scale. A drawing done to scale which can be measured off.

Tug A heavy duty vehicle used for towing caravans carrying mobile exhibitions.

Tungsten An element which glows white hot when an electrical current is passed through it.

TV monitor A special television set specifically for viewing type, disc or computer-generated information.

TV projection A method of projecting TV pictures using red, blue and green 'guns'.

Typeface The style, form and detailed shape of lettering; each different one named.

Typography The art or style of printing.

Ultraviolet Invisible light, damaging to coloured materials and photographs but useful for stimulating U/V sensitive materials to produce irridescent effects.

Unplaned Raw, sawn timber from the cutting mill.

Venue The common name for the place at which an exhibition is held.

Vertical space Space devoted to display, communication and circulation control.

Viewing angle The angle from which a display is best seen.

Visual A drawing done by a designer to give an impression of how an exhibition will look on completion.

Voids Dead areas where too many objects of minor interest are placed together – or none at all.

Wall In the exhibition context, usually plywood or hardboard on framing, or chipboard or some other patent board. Never load-bearing.

Wet mounted Stuck down using water-based glues.

Working drawing A drawing done by a designer or draught-sperson for a builder to work from.

Working model Same as an animated model. Usually applies to small scale replicas which work or operate like the real thing.

Workshop The place of work or factory of craftspeople or contractors.

World fair An exposition of the achievements of many countries in national pavilions.

Yellow Pages A directory of companies and businesses listed under professional, trade or craft names.

BIBLIOGRAPHY

Exhibition Design, edited by Misha Black, London: Architectural Press, 1950.

Exhibitions and Display, James Gardner and Caroline Heller, London: Batsford, 1960.

Directional Signing and Labelling in Libraries and Museums: a review of current theory and practice, Herbert Spencer and Linda Reynolds. Readability of Print Research Unit, Royal College of Art, London, September 1977.

The Great Exhibitions, John Allwood, London: Studio Vista (Cassell/Collier Macmillan), 1977.

Manual of Curatorship: a guide to museum practice, edited by John M A Thompson, London: Butterworth/The Museums Association, 1984 (includes a chapter on exhibition design by Giles Velarde).

On Display: a design grammar for museum exhibitions, Margaret Hall, London: Lund Humphries, 1987.

INDEX

Numbers in italic refer to illustrations